low-fat
pasta

low-fat
pasta

Over 150 inspirational and healthy step-by-step recipes for all occasions, shown in more than 160 tempting photographs

Edited by
Valerie Ferguson

southwater

This edition is published by Southwater, an imprint of Anness Publishing Ltd, Hermes House, 88–89 Blackfriars Road, London SE1 8HA; tel. 020 7401 2077; fax 020 7633 9499

www.southwaterbooks.com; www.annesspublishing.com

If you like the images in this book and would like to investigate using them for publishing, promotions or advertising, please visit our website www.practicalpictures.com for more information.

UK distributor: Book Trade Services; tel. 0116 2759086; fax 0116 2759090; uksales@booktradeservices.com; exportsales@booktradeservices.com
North American distributor: National Book Network; tel. 301 459 3366; fax 301 429 5746; www.nbnbooks.com
Australian distributor: Pan Macmillan Australia; tel. 1300 135 113; fax 1300 135 103; customer.service@macmillan.com.au
New Zealand distributor: David Bateman Ltd; tel. (09) 415 7664; fax (09) 415 8892

Publisher: Joanna Lorenz
Editor: Valerie Ferguson
Recipes contributed by: Catherine Atkinson, Alex Barker, Michelle Berriedale-Johnson, Angela Boggiano, Janet Brinkworth, Carla Capalbo, Kit Chan, Jacqueline Clark, Maxine Clarke, Frances Cleary, Trish Davies, Roz Denny, Patrizia Diemling, Matthew Drennan, Sarah Edmonds, Rafi Fernandez, Christine France, Sarah Gates, Shirley Gill, Nicola Graimes, Rosamund Grant, Rebekah Hassan, Deh-Ta Hsuing, Shehzad Husain, Christine Ingram, Judy Jackson, Masaki Ko, Lesley Mackley, Norma MacMillan, Sue Maggs, Kathy Man, Elizabeth Martin, Sallie Morris, Annie Nichols, Maggie Pannell, Katherine Richmond, Anne Sheasby, Jenny Stacey, Liz Trigg, Hilaire Walden, Laura Washburn, Steven Wheeler, Judy Williams, Jeni Wright
Photography: William Adams-Lingwood, Karl Adamson, Edward Allwright, David Armstrong, Steve Baxter, Nicki Dowey, James Duncan, John Freeman, Ian Garlick, Michelle Garrett, John Heseltine, Amanda Heywood, Janine Hosegood, David Jordan, Don Last, Patrick McLeavey, Thomas Odulate, Juliet Piddington, Peter Reilly
Designer: Carole Perks
Typesetter: Diane Pullen
Editorial Reader: Richard McGinlay
Production Controller: Pirong Wang

ETHICAL TRADING POLICY

Because of our ongoing ecological investment programme, you, as our customer, can have the pleasure and reassurance of knowing that a tree is being cultivated on your behalf to naturally replace the materials used to make the book you are holding. For further information about this scheme, go to www.annesspublishing.com/trees

A CIP catalogue record for this book is available from the British Library.

Previously published as part of a larger volume, *Pasta*

NOTES

For all recipes, quantities are given in both metric and imperial measures and, where appropriate, in standard cups and spoons. Follow one set of measures, but not a mixture, because they are not interchangeable.
Standard spoon and cup measures are level. 1 tsp = 5ml, 1 tbsp = 15ml, 1 cup = 250ml/8fl oz.
Australian standard tablespoons are 20ml. Australian readers should use 3 tsp in place of 1 tbsp for measuring small quantities.
American pints are 16fl oz/2 cups. American readers should use 20fl oz/2.5 cups in place of 1 pint when measuring liquids.
Electric oven temperatures in this book are for conventional ovens. When using a fan oven, the temperature will probably need to be reduced by about 10–20°C/20–40°F. Since ovens vary, you should check with your manufacturer's instruction book for guidance.
Medium (US large) eggs are used unless otherwise stated.
Main front cover image shows Spaghetti with Meatballs – for recipe, see page 64.

PUBLISHER'S NOTE

Although the advice and information in this book are believed to be accurate and true at the time of going to press, neither the authors nor the publisher can accept any legal responsibility or liability for any errors or omissions that may have been made nor for any inaccuracies nor for any loss, harm or injury that comes about from following instructions or advice in this book.

Contents

Introduction

Italians are passionate about their food and always enjoy spending time preparing, cooking and eating meals with family and friends. Food is one of their greatest pleasures and Italians are fortunate to be able to enjoy many regional variations in the dishes they eat. Pasta, a central part of Italian cuisine, is thought by many of us to be laden with calories and fat, but in fact it can be enjoyed as part of a healthy, low-fat cuisine.

Many traditional Italian ingredients such as the abundance of fresh Mediterranean sun-ripened vegetables, fresh herbs and the numerous different types of pasta are naturally low in

fat, making them ideal to enjoy as part of a low-fat eating plan. Quality and freshness of foods are both of great importance to the Italians and much of the fresh produce eaten is grown or produced locally. When it comes to cooking ingredients such as vegetables, they are often prepared in simple ways to bring out their delicious and natural flavours.

Olive oil is the primary fat used for cooking in Italy and it is also commonly used for dressing foods such as salads. Olive oil is a "healthier" type of fat which is high in monounsaturated fat and low in saturated fat, and so long as it is used in moderation, it can also be enjoyed as part of a low-fat diet.

Some other typical Italian ingredients, such as pancetta, salami, Parmesan and mozzarella, are high in fat but are easily substituted with lower-fat foods such as lean bacon and reduced-fat mozzarella, or, in many recipes, the quantity of the high-fat food can often simply be reduced to lower the fat content of the dish.

In Italy, pasta dishes form a large part of the cuisine, and the many varieties are ideal for a low-fat diet as they are naturally high in carbohydrates and low in fat, so long as the sauce served with the pasta dish is also low in fat!

Most of us eat fats in some form or another every day, and we all need a small amount of fat in our diet to maintain a healthy, balanced eating plan. However, most of us eat far too much fat and we should all be looking to reduce our overall fat intake, especially saturated fats.

Weight for weight, dietary fats supply far more energy than all the other nutrients in our diet, and if you eat a diet that is high in fat but don't exercise sufficiently to use up that energy, you will gain weight.

By cutting down on the amount of fat you eat and making easy changes to your diet, such as choosing the right types of fat, using low-fat and fat-free products whenever possible and making simple changes to the way you prepare

and cook food, you will soon be reducing your overall fat intake and enjoying a much healthier lifestyle – and you'll hardly notice the difference!

As you will see from this cookbook, it is certainly practicable to eat and enjoy pasta dishes as part of a low-fat eating plan. We have included some Asian noodle dishes as they offer variety and a distinctly different flavour, while still being low in fat. We provide lots of useful and informative advice, including an introduction to basic healthy eating guidelines: helpful hints and tips on low-fat and fat-free ingredients and low-fat or fat-free cooking techniques, and practical tips on how to reduce fat and saturated fat in your diet.

All the recipes in this cookbook are very low in fat – each containing 15 grams of fat or less per serving, some containing less than 5 grams of fat per serving.

You will be surprised and delighted at this tempting collection of recipes which ranges from soups and salads to main-course pasta and noodle dishes, with fish and seafood, poultry, meat and vegetables. All the recipes contain less fat than similar recipes and yet they are packed full of flavour and appeal. This inspirational cookbook with over 140 mouthwatering recipes will give you a valuable insight into low-fat cookery, and will enable you to enjoy food that is healthy, delicious and nutritious as well as being low in fat.

Fat & Calorie Counter

The following figures show the weight of fat (g) and the energy content per 90g/3½oz

Vegetables	Fat (g)	Energy
Artichokes, globe, boiled	0.2	24 Kcal/101 kj
Asparagus, boiled	0.6	25 Kcal/103 kj
Aubergines, raw	0.4	15 Kcal/64 kj
Broccoli, raw	0.9	33 Kcal/138 kj
Carrots, raw	0.9	35 Kcal/146 kj
Celery, raw	0.2	7 Kcal/29 kj
Courgettes, raw	0.4	18 Kcal/74 kj
Fennel, Florence, raw	0.2	12 Kcal/50 kj
Mushrooms, raw	0.4	13 Kcal/55 kj
Olives, in brine	11.0	103 Kcal/422 kj
Onions, raw	0.2	36 Kcal/150 kj
Peas, raw	1.5	83 Kcal/344 kj
Peppers, red, raw	0.4	32 Kcal/134 kj
Spinach, raw	0.8	25 Kcal/103 kj
Sweetcorn, tinned	1.1	110 Kcal/467 kj
Tomatoes, raw	0.3	17 Kcal/73 kj

Fruit, Nuts & Seeds		
Apples, eating, raw	0.1	47 Kcal/199 kj
Oranges	0.1	37 Kcal/158 kj
Peanuts	13.3	150 Kcal/623 kj
Pine nuts	68.6	688 Kcal/2840 kj
Walnuts	68.5	688 Kcal/2840 kj

Pasta & Noodles		
Egg noodles, boiled	0.4	56 Kcal/238 kj
Pasta, white, cooked	0.7	104 Kcal/437 kj
Pasta, wholemeal, cooked	0.9	113 Kcal/475 kj

Cereals, Beans & Pulses		
Bread, white	1.9	235 Kcal/1002 kj
Chick-peas	0.7	29 Kcal/122 kj
Flour, plain, white	1.2	307 Kcal/1305 kj
Green and brown lentils, cooked	0.7	105 Kcal/446 kj
Red kidney beans, canned	0.6	100 Kcal/424 kj
Sesame seeds	145	150 Kcal/618 kj
Soy sauce	0.0	11 Kcal/46 kj
Tofu/beancurd	3.8	63 Kcal/263 kj

Fish & Shellfish		
Anchovies, canned in oil	19.9	280 Kcal/1165 kj
Clams, canned in natural juice	0.6	77 Kcal/325 kj
Crab, canned in brine	0.5	77 Kcal/325 kj
Prawns, boiled	0.9	99 Kcal/418 kj
Salmon, raw	11.0	180 Kcal/750 kj
Salmon, smoked	4.5	142 Kcal/598 kj
Salmon, steamed	11.9	194 Kcal/812 kj
Scallops, queen, steamed	1.4	118 Kcal/496 kj
Squid, raw	1.7	81 Kcal/344 kj
Trout, cooked	1.4	34 Kcal/141 kj
Tuna, canned in brine	0.6	99 Kcal/422 kj

Meat & Poultry		
Bacon rashers, lean back, grilled	5.2	172 Kcal/722 kj
Beef mince, extra lean, stewed	6.6	121 Kcal/508 kj
Beef, topside, lean, roast	4.4	156 Kcal/655 kj
Chicken breast, no skin, roast	1.1	153 Kcal/643 kj
Chicken livers, fried	8.0	152 Kcal/630 kj
Duck, meat only, roast	10.4	195 Kcal/819 kj
Lamb, leg, lean, roast	9.6	210 Kcal/822 kj
Pork, leg, lean, roast	6.9	185 Kcal/777 kj
Sausage pork, reduced-fat, grilled	12.4	207 Kcal/863 kj
Turkey, meat only, roast	2.0	153 Kcal/643 kj

Dairy, Fats & Oils		
Butter	81.7	737 Kcal/722 kj
Cream cheese	47.4	439 Kcal/508 kj
Curd cheese	11.7	173 Kcal/655 kj
Eggs, whole, raw	10.8	147 Kcal/643 kj
Egg white, raw	Trace	36 Kcal/819 kj
Egg yolk, raw	30.5	339 Kcal/822 kj
Fromage frais, plain	7.1	113 Kcal/777 kj
Fromage frais, very low-fat	0.2	58 Kcal/643 kj
Groundnut/Vegetable/Sesame oil	89.9	809 Kcal/3326 kj
Low-fat cottage cheese	1.4	78 Kcal/722 kj
Low-fat crème fraîche	15.0	165 Kcal/508 kj
Low-fat soft cheese	Trace	74 Kcal/655 kj
Low-fat spread	40.5	390 Kcal/605 kj
Low-fat yogurt, natural	0.8	56 Kcal/819 kj
Milk, skimmed	0.1	33 Kcal/822 kj
Olive oil	99.9	899 Kcal/777 kj
Parmesan cheese	32.7	452 Kcal/643 kj
Ricotta cheese	11.0	144 Kcal/599 kj
Very low-fat spread	25.0	273 Kcal/643 kj

Alcohol & Sugar		
Red wine	0.0	17 Kcal/71 kj
White wine	0.0	17 Kcal/71 kj
White sugar	0.0	355 Kcal/1512 kj

Types of Pasta

There are at least 200 different types of pasta - and there can sometimes seem to be about ten times as many names.

Most pasta is made from durum wheat flour, which is quite hard and does not go soggy when cooked. Dried pasta may simply have been mixed with water or may also contain egg, while fresh pasta – *pasta all'uova* – always contains egg. As a result of a growing interest in healthy foods, wholemeal pasta, which has a rich brown colour, has become increasingly popular. Buckwheat pasta, which is an even darker colour, is also available and is suitable for people on a gluten-free diet. Pasta may be coloured and flavoured with a range of ingredients. The most common additions are tomatoes and spinach, but beetroot, saffron, herbs, wild mushrooms and cuttlefish ink are also widely used.

There are no hard-and-fast rules about which shapes to serve with particular sauces, but some shapes do work better than others. The recipes in this book include one or more recommendations, but you can substitute a shape of your choice.

Hollow Pasta
These include penne, fusilli, macaroni, farfalle, rigatoni, orecchiette, rotelli, tortiglioni, chifferi rigati, ruote and mezze. Try these with robust sauces, such as cheese, tomato and vegetable.

Long Pasta
These include spaghetti, linguine, tagliatelle, tagliarini and fettuccine. Some are flat ribbons, while others are hollow tubes. All go well with smooth and creamy sauces and vegetable sauces with finely chopped ingredients.

Filled Pasta
These include ravioli, cappelletti and tortelloni. These are good with simple sauces, such as tomato.

Pasta for Baking
These include very delicate shapes, such as risi and orzi, as well as larger ones for more robust dishes – tubetti, conchiglie, cannelloni and lasagne, for example.

Above: A selection of the many different types of pasta.

Basic Pasta Dough
Serves 3–4
200g/7 oz/1¾ cups plain flour (Italian tipo 00 is the best if you can find it)
pinch of salt
2 eggs
10ml/2 tsp cold water

Variations:
Tomato: add 20ml/4 tsp concentrated tomato purée to the eggs before mixing.
Spinach: add 115g/4oz frozen spinach, thawed and squeezed of excess moisture. Combine or process with the eggs, before adding the mixture to the flour.
Herb: add 45ml/3 tbsp finely chopped fresh herbs to the eggs before mixing the dough.
Wholemeal: use 50g/2oz plain flour and 150g/5oz wholemeal flour. Add an extra 10ml/2 tsp cold water.

Making Pasta by Hand

1 Sift the flour and salt on to a clean work surface and make a well in the centre with your hand.

2 Put the eggs and water into the well. Using a fork, beat the eggs gently together, then gradually draw in the flour from the sides, combining to make a thick pasta.

3 When the mixture becomes too stiff to use a fork, use your hands to continue to combine to form a firm dough. Knead the dough for about 5 minutes, until it is smooth.

4 Wrap the dough in clear film and leave it to rest for 20–30 minutes.

SOUPS & SALADS

Puglia-style Minestrone

Ricotta salata is the traditional garnish for this simple soup. You don't need to use much; even a small sprinkling boosts the flavour.

Serves 4
2 skinless, boneless chicken thighs
1 onion, quartered lengthways
1 carrot, roughly chopped
1 celery stick, roughly chopped
a few black peppercorns
1 small handful mixed fresh
  herbs, such as parsley
  and thyme
1 chicken stock cube
1.2 litres/2 pints/5 cups water
50g/2oz/½ cup dried tubetti
salt and freshly ground
  black pepper
25g/1oz ricotta salata, coarsely
  grated or crumbled and 30ml/
  2 tbsp fresh mint leaves,
  to serve

1 Put the chicken thighs in a large saucepan. Add the onion, carrot, celery, peppercorns and herbs, then crumble in the stock cube. Pour in the water and bring to the boil.

2 Lower the heat, half cover the pan and simmer gently for about 1 hour. Remove the pan from the heat. Leave the liquid to cool, then strain it into a clean large saucepan. Discard the flavouring ingredients. Blot the surface with kitchen paper to remove surface fat.

3 Cut the chicken into bite-size pieces and set aside.

4 Bring the stock in the pan to the boil, add the pasta and simmer, stirring until only just al dente.

5 Add the pieces of chicken and heat through for a few minutes. Taste for seasoning. Serve hot in warmed bowls, sprinkled with the ricotta salata and mint leaves.

Cook's Tip
Ricotta salata is a salted and dried version of ricotta, which can easily be crumbled. If it is not available, crumbled feta cheese can be used instead.

Pasta Soup with Chicken Livers

A soup that can be served as either a first or main course. The fried chicken livers are so delicious that even if you do not normally like them, you will relish them in this soup.

Serves 4–6
115g/4oz/⅔ cup chicken livers,
  thawed if frozen
3 sprigs each fresh parsley,
  marjoram and sage
leaves from 1 fresh thyme sprig
5–6 fresh basil leaves
15ml/1 tbsp olive oil
4 garlic cloves, crushed
15–30ml/1–2 tbsp dry
  white wine
2 x 300g/11oz cans condensed
  chicken consommé
225g/8oz/2 cups frozen peas
50g/2oz/½ cup dried farfalle
2–3 spring onions,
  sliced diagonally
salt and freshly ground
  black pepper

1 Cut the chicken livers into small pieces with scissors. Finely chop the herbs. Heat the olive oil in a frying pan, add the garlic and herbs, season with salt and pepper to taste, and fry gently for a few minutes.

2 Add the chicken livers, increase the heat to high and stir-fry for a few minutes, until they change colour and become dry. Pour over the wine, cook until it evaporates, then remove the livers from the heat and taste for seasoning.

3 Tip both cans of condensed chicken consommé into a large saucepan and add water to the condensed soup as directed on the labels. Add an extra can of water, then stir in a little salt and pepper to taste and bring to the boil.

4 Add the frozen peas to the pan and simmer for about 5 minutes, then add the pasta and bring the soup back to the boil, stirring. Allow to simmer, stirring frequently, until the pasta is only just al dente.

5 Add the fried chicken livers and spring onions, and heat through for 2–3 minutes. Taste for seasoning. Serve hot, in warmed bowls.

Broccoli, Anchovy & Pasta Soup

In this tasty soup, broccoli and anchovies make excellent partners for pretty little orecchiette.

Serves 4
30ml/2 tbsp olive oil
1 small onion, finely chopped
1 garlic clove, finely chopped
1/4–1/3 fresh red chilli, seeded and finely chopped
2 drained canned anchovies
200ml/7fl oz/scant 1 cup passata
45ml/3 tbsp dry white wine
1.2 litres/2 pints/5 cups vegetable stock
300g/11oz/2 cups broccoli florets
200g/7oz/1¾ cups dried orecchiette
salt and freshly ground black pepper
freshly grated Pecorino cheese, to serve

1 Heat the olive oil in a large, heavy-based saucepan. Add the onion, garlic, chilli and anchovies and cook over a low heat, stirring constantly, for 5–6 minutes.

2 Add the passata and wine, and season with salt and pepper to taste. Bring to the boil, cover the pan, then cook over a low heat, stirring occasionally, for 12–15 minutes.

3 Pour in the stock. Bring to the boil, then add the broccoli florets and simmer for about 5 minutes. Add the pasta and bring back to the boil, stirring.

4 Lower the heat and simmer, stirring frequently, until the pasta is al dente. Taste for seasoning and adjust, if necessary. Serve the soup hot, in warmed bowls, and hand around the grated Pecorino cheese separately.

> **Cook's Tip**
> Salted dried anchovies have a better flavour and texture than canned anchovies, but are not so widely available. If using them, rinse thoroughly in cold water and pat dry on kitchen paper first. If they are still too salty, then soak them in milk for about 30 minutes, rinse in cold water and pat dry.

Clam & Pasta Soup

This soup is based on the classic pasta dish – spaghetti alle vongole – but uses store-cupboard ingredients. Serve it with hot focaccia or ciabatta for an informal supper with friends.

Serves 4
30ml/2 tbsp olive oil
1 large onion, finely chopped
2 garlic cloves, crushed
400g/14oz can chopped tomatoes
15ml/1 tbsp sun-dried tomato purée
5ml/1 tsp granulated sugar
5ml/1 tsp dried mixed herbs
about 750ml/1¼ pints/3 cups fish or vegetable stock
150ml/¼ pint/⅔ cup red wine
50g/2oz/½ cup small dried pasta shapes
150g/5oz jar or can clams in natural juice
30ml/2 tbsp finely chopped fresh flat leaf parsley, plus a few whole leaves, to garnish
salt and freshly ground black pepper

1 Heat the oil in a large saucepan. Cook the onion gently, stirring frequently, for 5 minutes, until softened.

2 Add the garlic, tomatoes, sun-dried tomato pureé, sugar, herbs, stock and wine, and season with salt and pepper to taste. Bring to the boil. Lower the heat, half cover the pan and simmer for 10 minutes, stirring occasionally.

3 Add the pasta and continue simmering, uncovered, until al dente. Stir occasionally, to prevent the pasta shapes from sticking together.

4 Add the clams and their juice to the soup and heat through for 3–4 minutes, adding more stock if required. Do not let the soup boil or the clams will be tough.

5 Remove from the heat, stir in the parsley and taste the soup for seasoning. Serve hot, sprinkled with coarsely ground black pepper and parsley leaves.

Sweetcorn Chowder with Conchigliette

Chowders are always wonderfully satisfying, and this one is no exception. It is low in fat, but high on the flavour stakes.

Serves 6–8
1 small green pepper, diced
450g/1lb potatoes, peeled and diced
350g/12oz/2 cups drained canned or frozen sweetcorn
1 onion, chopped
1 celery stick, chopped
bouquet garni (bay leaf, parsley stalks and thyme)
600ml/1 pint/2½ cups chicken stock
300ml/½ pint/1¼ cups skimmed milk
50g/2oz/½ cup dried conchigliette
150g/5oz smoked turkey rashers, diced
salt and freshly ground black pepper
bread sticks, to serve

1 Put the diced green pepper in a bowl and pour over the boiling water to cover. Leave to stand for 2 minutes. Drain, rinse and drain again.

2 Put the green pepper into a large, heavy-based saucepan and add the potatoes, sweetcorn, onion, celery, bouquet garni and stock. Bring to the boil, lower the heat, cover and simmer for 20 minutes until tender.

3 Add the milk, then season with salt and pepper to taste. Process half of the soup in a food processor or blender and return it to the pan. Add the conchigliette and simmer over a low heat until the pasta is *al dente*.

4 Meanwhile, fry the diced turkey rashers quickly in a non-stick frying pan for 2–3 minutes. Stir them into the soup. Serve in warmed bowls, with bread sticks.

Pasta & Lentil Soup

Small brown lentils are partnered with pasta shapes in this wholesome soup, which is delicately flavoured with fresh herbs.

Serves 4–6
225g/8oz/1 cup brown lentils
30ml/2 tbsp olive oil
2 rindless lean back bacon rashers, diced
1 onion, finely chopped
1 celery stick, finely chopped
1 carrot, finely chopped
2 litres/3½ pints/8 cups chicken stock or water, or a combination
1 fresh sage leaf or a pinch of dried sage
1 fresh thyme sprig or 1.5ml/ ¼ tsp dried thyme
175g/6oz/1½ cups ditalini or other small soup pasta
salt and freshly ground black pepper
flat leaf parsley, to garnish

1 Pick over the lentils and remove any debris, such as small stones. Place the lentils in a bowl, pour over cold water to cover, and soak for 2–3 hours. Drain, rinse under cold running water and drain well again.

2 Heat the oil in a large saucepan and sauté the bacon for 2–3 minutes. Add the onion, and cook gently until it softens.

3 Stir in the celery and carrot, and cook for 5 minutes more, stirring frequently. Add the lentils, stirring well.

4 Pour in the stock or water and the herbs, then bring the soup to the boil. Cook over a medium heat for about 1 hour or until the lentils are tender. Add salt and pepper to taste.

5 Stir in the pasta, and cook until it is *al dente*. Allow the soup to stand for a few minutes before serving garnished with parsley.

Cook's Tip
If you use young organic vegetables, their flavour will probably be intense enough to make the addition of stock unnecessary. Just use water.

Chicken Noodle Soup

Just like Grandma used to make, this is comfort food, pure and simple.

Serves 8
1 chicken, about 1.4kg/3lb, cut
   into pieces
2 onions, quartered
1 parsnip, quartered
2 carrots, quartered
2.5ml/ ½ tsp salt
1 bay leaf
2 allspice berries
4 black peppercorns
1.5 litres/2½ pints/6 cups water
115g/4oz very thin egg noodles
fresh dill sprigs, to garnish

1 Put the chicken pieces, onions, parsnip, carrots, salt, bay leaf, allspice berries and peppercorns in a large saucepan.

2 Add the measured water. Bring to the boil, skimming the surface frequently, then lower the heat and simmer for about 1½ hours, skimming occasionally.

3 Strain the stock into a large bowl. Discard the vegetables and flavourings in the strainer, but remove the chicken pieces and set them aside.

4 When the chicken pieces are cool enough to handle, skin them and chop the flesh into bite-size pieces. Put these in a bowl. When both the chicken and the stock are cold, cover both the bowls and put them in the fridge overnight.

5 Next day, remove the solidified fat from the surface of the chilled stock. Pour it into a saucepan and bring to the boil.

6 Add the chicken and noodles, and cook until the noodles are *al dente*. Serve in warmed bowls, garnished with dill sprigs.

> **Cook's Tip**
> *If you haven't got time to chill the chicken stock in the fridge overnight, just blot the surface several times with kitchen paper to remove the excess fat.*

Cock-a-Noodle Soup

Take a tasty trip to the Far East, with this quick and easy Chinese-style soup.

Serves 4–6
15ml/1 tbsp corn oil
4 spring onions, roughly chopped
225g/8oz skinless, boneless
   chicken breasts, cut into
   small cubes
1.2 litres/2 pints/5 cups
   chicken stock
15ml/1 tbsp soy sauce
115g/4oz/1 cup frozen
   sweetcorn niblets
115g/4oz medium egg noodles
salt and freshly ground
   black pepper
1 carrot, thinly sliced lengthways,
   to garnish

1 Heat the oil in a saucepan and fry the spring onions and chicken until the meat is evenly browned.

2 Add the stock and the soy sauce and bring to the boil, then stir in the sweetcorn.

3 Add the noodles, breaking them up roughly. Taste the soup and add salt and pepper if needed.

4 Use small cutters to stamp out shapes from the thin slices of carrot. Add them to the soup. Simmer for 5 minutes. Serve in warmed bowls.

Summer Minestrone

This brightly coloured, fresh-tasting soup makes the most of summer vegetables. Peperini are very tiny, but you could use larger pasta shapes if preferred.

Serves 4
15ml/1 tbsp olive oil
1 large onion, finely chopped
15ml/1 tbsp tomato purée
450g/1lb ripe Italian plum
   tomatoes, peeled and
   finely chopped
225g/8oz green courgettes,
   trimmed and roughly chopped
225g/8oz yellow courgettes,
   trimmed and roughly chopped
3 waxy new potatoes, diced
2 garlic cloves, crushed
about 1.2 litres/2 pints/5 cups
   light chicken stock or water
25g/1oz/ ¼ cup peperini
60ml/4 tbsp shredded fresh basil
salt and freshly ground
   black pepper
grated Parmesan cheese,
   to serve (optional)

1 Heat the oil in a large saucepan. Add the onion and cook over a low heat, stirring constantly, for about 5 minutes, until softened. Stir in the tomato purée, chopped tomatoes, courgettes, diced potatoes and garlic. Mix well and cook gently for 10 minutes, uncovered, shaking the pan frequently to stop the vegetables from sticking to the base.

2 Pour in the stock or water and bring to the boil. Add the peperini, lower the heat, half cover the pan and simmer gently for 10–15 minutes or until both the vegetables and the pasta are just tender. Add more stock if necessary.

3 Remove the pan from the heat and stir in the basil. Taste for seasoning and adjust, if necessary. Serve hot, sprinkled with a little Parmesan, if you like.

Chicken Vermicelli Soup with Egg Shreds

This soup is quick and easy to make, and very versatile. Add extra ingredients if you like, such as spring onions, mushrooms, prawns or chopped salami.

Serves 4–6

3 large eggs
30ml/2 tbsp chopped fresh
    coriander or parsley
1.5 litres/2½ pints/6 cups
    chicken stock
115g/4oz/1 cup dried vermicelli
    or capelli d'angelo, broken into
    short lengths
115g/4oz cooked chicken
    breast, shredded
salt and freshly ground
    black pepper

1 First make the egg shreds. Whisk the eggs together in a small bowl and stir in the coriander or parsley.

2 Heat a small non-stick frying pan and pour in about 45ml/ 3 tbsp of the egg mixture, swirling to cover the base, and make a thin pancake. Cook until just set. Slide the pancake on to a plate and repeat until all the mixture is used up.

3 Roll each pancake up and, using a sharp knife, slice thinly crossways into shreds. Set aside.

4 Bring the stock to the boil and add the pasta. Cook until it is almost *al dente*, then add the chicken and season with salt and pepper to taste. Heat through for 2–3 minutes, then stir in the egg shreds. Serve immediately.

> **Variation**
> To make a Thai variation, use Chinese rice noodles instead of vermicelli. Stir 2.5ml/½ tsp dried lemon grass, two small whole fresh green chillies and 60ml/4 tbsp coconut milk into the chicken stock. Add four thinly sliced spring onions and plenty of chopped fresh coriander.

Chicken & Stellette Soup

Little pasta stars look very attractive in this tasty soup, which is sufficiently sophisticated to serve at a dinner party, yet has plenty of child appeal if you omit the wine.

Serves 4–6

900ml/1½ pints/3¾ cups
    chicken stock
1 bay leaf
4 spring onions, sliced
225g/8oz/3 cups button
    mushrooms, sliced
50g/2oz/½ cup stellette
115g/4oz cooked, skinless chicken
    breast, thinly sliced
150ml/ ¼ pint/ ⅔ cup dry
    white wine
15ml/1 tbsp chopped
    fresh parsley
salt and freshly ground
    black pepper

1 Put the stock and bay leaf into a pan and bring to the boil over a medium heat.

2 Add the spring onions, mushrooms and pasta. Lower the heat, cover and simmer for 7–8 minutes.

3 Just before serving, add the chicken, wine and parsley, and season to taste. Heat through for 2–3 minutes, then serve in warmed bowls.

> **Variations**
> Any small soup pasta can be substituted for stellette – old-fashioned alphabet shapes are very popular with young children and will amuse nostalgic adults. "Safari" pasta is also fun. Leave out the wine when making the soup for youngsters, and add a little extra stock instead.

Tiny Pasta in Broth

Serve this quick and easy soup with warm bread rolls for an after-theatre supper, or as a light starter before a hearty main course.

Serves 4
1.2 litres/2 pints/5 cups beef stock
75g/3oz/ $^3/_4$ cup dried funghetti or other tiny soup pasta

2 pieces drained bottled roasted red pepper
salt and freshly ground black pepper

To serve
coarsely shaved Parmesan cheese (optional)
warm bread rolls

1 Bring the beef stock to the boil in a large saucepan. Season with salt and pepper to taste, then drop in the dried pasta. Stir well and bring the stock back to the boil.

2 Lower the heat to a simmer and cook until the pasta is *al dente*. Stir frequently.

3 Finely dice the pieces of roasted pepper. Divide them equally among four warmed soup plates. Taste the soup for seasoning and adjust, if necessary. Ladle into the soup plates and serve immediately, with shavings of Parmesan handed separately, if using, and a basket of warm rolls.

Cook's Tip
Stock cubes are not really suitable for a recipe like this in which the flavour of the broth is crucially important. If you have insufficient time to make your own stock, use two 300g/11oz cans of good-quality condensed beef consommé, adding water as instructed on the labels.

Meatball & Pasta Soup

You can make a meal of this marvellous soup, and it is very popular with children.

Serves 4
2 x 300g/11oz cans condensed beef consommé
90g/3 $^1/_2$ oz dried fidelini or spaghettini
fresh flat leaf parsley to garnish
freshly grated Parmesan cheese, to serve (optional)

For the meatballs
1 very thick slice of white bread, crusts removed
30ml/2 tbsp milk
225g/8oz minced beef
1 garlic clove, crushed
15ml/1 tbsp freshly grated Parmesan cheese
30–45ml/2–3 tbsp fresh flat leaf parsley leaves, coarsely chopped
1 egg
nutmeg
salt and freshly ground black pepper

1 First, make the meatballs. Break the bread into a small bowl, add the milk and set aside to soak. Meanwhile, put the minced beef, garlic, Parmesan, parsley and egg in another large bowl. Grate fresh nutmeg liberally over the top and add salt and pepper to taste.

2 Squeeze the bread with your hands to remove as much milk as possible, then add the bread to the meatball mixture and mix together well with your hands. Wash your hands, rinse them under cold water, then form the mixture into tiny balls about the size of small marbles.

3 Tip both cans of consommé into a large saucepan, add water as directed on the labels, then add an extra can of water. Stir in salt and pepper to taste and bring to the boil.

4 Drop in the meatballs, then break the pasta into small pieces and add it to the soup. Bring to the boil, stirring gently. Lower the heat and simmer, stirring frequently, until the pasta is *al dente*. Taste for seasoning and adjust, if necessary. Serve hot in warmed soup bowls, sprinkled with the parsley and freshly grated Parmesan cheese, if using.

Roasted Tomato & Pasta Soup

Roasting tomatoes really brings out their flavour, and the soup has a wonderful smoky taste.

Serves 4

450g/1lb ripe Italian plum
    tomatoes, halved lengthways
1 large red pepper, quartered
    lengthways and seeded
1 large red onion,
    quartered lengthways
2 whole garlic cloves, unpeeled
15ml/1 tbsp olive oil
1.2 litres/2 pints/5 cups vegetable
    stock or water
good pinch of granulated sugar
90g/3½oz/scant 1 cup dried
    tubetti or other small
    pasta shapes
salt and freshly ground
    black pepper
fresh basil leaves,
    to garnish

1 Preheat the oven to 190°C/375°F/Gas 5. Spread out the tomatoes, red pepper, onion and unpeeled garlic cloves in a roasting tin. Drizzle with the olive oil. Roast for 30–40 minutes, until the vegetables are soft and charred, stirring and turning them halfway through the cooking time.

2 Tip the vegetables into a food processor, add about 250ml/8fl oz/1 cup of the stock or water and process until puréed. Scrape into a sieve placed over a large saucepan and press the purée through into the pan.

3 Add the remaining stock or water, and the sugar, and season with salt and pepper to taste. Bring to the boil over a medium heat, stirring constantly.

4 Add the pasta and cook, stirring frequently, until it is al dente. Taste for seasoning. Serve hot in warmed bowls, garnished with the fresh basil leaves.

Cook's Tip
The soup can be frozen without the pasta. Thaw it thoroughly, pour it into a pan and bring it to the boil before adding the pasta.

Farmhouse Soup

Swedes and turnips are often forgotten by modern cooks, which is a shame, for they have excellent flavour. Try them in this chunky, rustic main-meal soup.

Serves 4

30ml/2 tbsp olive oil
1 onion, roughly chopped
3 carrots, cut into large chunks
1 turnip, about 200g/7oz, cut into
    large chunks
about 175g/6oz swede, cut into
    large chunks
400g/14oz can chopped
    Italian tomatoes
15ml/1 tbsp tomato purée
5ml/1 tsp dried mixed herbs
5ml/1 tsp dried oregano
50g/2oz/½ cup dried peppers,
    washed and thinly
    sliced (optional)
1.5 litres/2½ pints/6 cups
    vegetable stock or water
50g/2oz/½ cup dried conchiglie
    or other pasta shapes
400g/14oz can red kidney beans,
    rinsed and drained
30ml/2 tbsp chopped fresh flat
    leaf parsley
salt and freshly ground
    black pepper
freshly grated Parmesan
    cheese (optional) and crusty
    bread, to serve

1 Heat the olive oil in a large, heavy-based saucepan, add the onion and cook over a low heat, stirring occasionally, for about 5 minutes until softened.

2 Add the carrots, turnip, swede, canned tomatoes, tomato purée, dried mixed herbs, oregano and dried peppers, if using. Season with salt and pepper to taste. Pour in the stock or water and bring to the boil over a medium heat. Stir well, cover, lower the heat and simmer, stirring occasionally, for 30 minutes, until the vegetables are tender.

3 Add the pasta and bring to the boil, stirring constantly. Lower the heat and simmer until the pasta is only just al dente.

4 Stir in the kidney beans. Heat through for 2–3 minutes, then stir in the parsley. Serve hot in warmed soup bowls, with Parmesan handed separately, if using, and thick slices of crusty bread.

Cook's Tip
Packets of dried Italian peppers are sold in many supermarkets and in delicatessens. They are piquant and firm with a "meaty" bite to them, which makes them ideal for adding substance and concentrated flavour to soups.

Variation
Use two leeks instead of the onion and borlotti beans instead of the kidney beans. Virtually any small pasta shapes are suitable; chunky ones, such as pipe rigate or penne rigate work best.

Minestrone with Pasta & Beans

This tasty soup is made using canned beans, so is ideal for a spur-of-the-moment lunch invitation. A small amount of pancetta gives depth to the flavour.

Serves 4
15ml/1 tbsp olive oil
50g/2oz pancetta, rind removed, roughly chopped
2–3 celery sticks, finely chopped
3 carrots, finely chopped
1 onion, finely chopped
1–2 garlic cloves, crushed
2 x 400g/14oz cans chopped tomatoes
about 1 litre/1³⁄₄ pints/4 cups chicken stock
400g/14oz can cannellini beans, drained and rinsed
50g/2oz/¹⁄₂ cup short-cut macaroni
30–60ml/2–4 tbsp chopped flat leaf parsley, to taste
salt and freshly ground black pepper
shaved Parmesan cheese, to serve (optional)

1 Heat the olive oil in a large, heavy-based saucepan. Add the pancetta, celery, carrots and onion, and cook over a low heat for 5 minutes, stirring constantly, until the vegetables have begun to soften.

2 Add the garlic and tomatoes, breaking the tomatoes up well with a wooden spoon. Pour in the chicken stock. Season with salt and pepper to taste and bring to the boil. Half cover the pan, lower the heat and simmer gently for about 20 minutes, until the vegetables are soft.

3 Add the cannellini beans to the pan, together with the macaroni. Bring to the boil again. Cover, lower the heat and continue to simmer for about 20 minutes more, until the pasta is *al dente*.

4 Check the consistency of the soup and add a little more stock, if necessary. Stir in the parsley. Taste and adjust the seasoning, if necessary.

5 Serve hot in warmed soup bowls, sprinkling each portion with a few shavings of Parmesan cheese, if using.

Clear Vegetable Soup

The success of this clear soup depends on the quality of the stock, so it is best to use home-made vegetable stock, if possible, rather than stock cubes. Otherwise, you could use a good-quality canned bouillon.

Serves 4
1 small carrot
1 baby leek
1 celery stick
50g/2oz green cabbage
900ml/1¹⁄₂ pints/3³⁄₄ cups vegetable stock
1 bay leaf
115g/4oz/1 cup drained cooked cannellini beans
25g/1oz/¹⁄₄ cup dried soup pasta, such as tiny shells, bows, stars or elbows
salt and freshly ground black pepper
snipped fresh chives, to garnish

1 Cut the carrot, leek and celery into 5cm/2in long strips. Slice the cabbage very finely.

2 Put the stock and bay leaf into a large, heavy-based saucepan and bring to the boil over a medium heat. Add the strips of carrot, leek and celery, lower the heat, cover the pan and simmer for 6 minutes.

3 Add the cabbage, cannellini beans and pasta shapes. Stir well to mix, then simmer, uncovered, for a further 4–5 minutes, or until all the vegetables are tender and the pasta is *al dente*.

4 Remove and discard the bay leaf, and season the soup to taste with salt and pepper. Ladle into four warmed soup bowls and garnish with the snipped chives. Serve immediately.

> **Variations**
> Use drained and rinsed canned cannellini beans to save time, if you like. Other beans that would also go well in this soup include flageolets, borlotti or haricots. You could also substitute a shallot for the leek, if liked.

Haricot Bean Soup with Pasta Shells

Soup you can almost stand a spoon in – that's what you get when you make this wonderful winter warmer.

Serves 6
175g/6oz/1½ cups dried haricot
    beans, soaked overnight in cold
    water to cover
1.75 litres/3 pints/7 cups unsalted
    vegetable stock or water
115g/4oz/1 cup dried medium
    pasta shells
60ml/4 tbsp olive oil, plus
    extra to serve
2 garlic cloves, crushed
60ml/4 tbsp chopped
    fresh parsley
salt and freshly ground
    black pepper

1 Drain the beans and place them in a large saucepan. Add the stock or water. Bring to the boil, then lower the heat and simmer, half-covered, for 2–2½ hours, or until tender.

2 Scoop half the beans and a little of their cooking liquid into a blender or food processor. Process to a purée, then scrape this back into the pan. Stir well and add extra water or stock if the soup seems too thick.

3 Bring the soup back to the boil. Stir in the pasta, lower the heat and simmer gently until *al dente*.

4 Heat the olive oil in a small pan. Add the garlic and fry over a low heat until golden. Stir into the soup with the parsley, and season well with salt and pepper. Ladle into warmed bowls and drizzle each with a little extra olive oil. Serve immediately.

> **Cook's Tip**
> *You can reduce the soaking time for the beans by putting them in a saucepan, covering with cold water and bringing very slowly to the boil over a very low heat. Then boil for 2 minutes, remove from the heat, cover and leave to soak for 1 hour.*

Tomato, Borlotti & Pasta Soup

This peasant soup is very thick. It should always be made with dried or fresh beans, never canned ones.

Serves 4–6
300g/11oz/1½ cups dried
    borlotti or cannellini beans,
    soaked overnight in water
    to cover
400g/14oz can
    chopped tomatoes
3 garlic cloves, crushed
2 bay leaves
pinch of coarsely ground
    black pepper
30ml/2 tbsp olive oil
750ml/1¼ pints/3 cups water
10ml/2 tsp tomato purée
10ml/2 tsp salt
200g/7oz/1¾ cups dried ditalini
    or other small pasta shapes
45ml/3 tbsp chopped
    fresh parsley
freshly grated Parmesan cheese,
    to serve (optional)

1 Drain the beans, rinse under cold water, then place them in a large saucepan. Pour over fresh water to cover. Bring to the boil and boil hard for 10 minutes. Drain, rinse and drain again.

2 Return the beans to the pan. Add enough water to cover them by 2.5cm/1in. Stir in the tomatoes, garlic, bay leaves, black pepper and oil. Bring to the boil, then simmer for 1½–2 hours, or until the beans are tender. If necessary, add more water.

3 Remove and discard the bay leaves. Scoop out about half of the bean mixture and process to a purée in a food processor. Stir it back into the pan. Add the measured water and tomato purée, then bring the soup to the boil.

4 Add the salt and the pasta. Cook, stirring occasionally, until the pasta is *al dente*. Stir in the parsley. Allow to stand for at least 10 minutes before serving in warmed bowls. Serve with grated Parmesan passed separately, if using.

Crab & Egg Noodle Broth

This delicious broth takes only minutes to make and is both nutritious and filling.

Serves 4

75g/3oz fine egg noodles
25g/1oz/2 tbsp butter
1 small bunch spring
  onions, chopped
1 celery stick, sliced
1 carrot, cut into batons
1.2 litres/2 pints/5 cups
  chicken stock
60ml/4 tbsp dry sherry
115g/4oz fresh or thawed frozen
  white crab meat, flaked
pinch of celery salt
pinch of cayenne pepper
10ml/2 tsp lemon juice
1 small bunch fresh coriander or
  flat leaf parsley, to garnish

1 Bring a large saucepan of salted water to the boil. Toss in the egg noodles and cook according to the instructions on the packet. Drain, cool under cold running water and leave immersed in water until required.

2 Heat the butter in another large pan, add the spring onions, celery and carrot, cover and cook the vegetables over a gentle heat for 3–4 minutes, until softened.

3 Add the chicken stock and sherry, bring to the boil, then lower the heat and cook for 5 minutes more.

4 Drain the noodles and add to the broth, together with the crab meat. Season to taste with celery salt and cayenne pepper, and sharpen with the lemon juice. Return to a simmer.

5 Ladle the broth into warmed shallow soup plates, scatter with roughly chopped coriander or parsley and serve.

Cook's Tip
For the best flavour, buy a freshly cooked crab and remove the meat yourself. Frozen crab meat, available from supermarkets, is a good substitute, but avoid canned crab, as this tastes rather bland and has a slightly soggy texture.

Variation
You could use other vegetables in season for this soup. Julienne strips of celeriac, broccoli spears or cauliflower florets would also work well.

Spicy Prawn & Noodle Soup

Diners spoon noodles into their bowls, followed by the accompaniments before ladling in the broth.

Serves 4–6

150g/5oz rice vermicelli, soaked
  in warm water until soft
25g/1oz/¼ cup raw cashew
  nuts, chopped
3 shallots, sliced
5cm/2in piece of lemon
  grass, shredded
2 garlic cloves, crushed
15ml/1 tbsp vegetable oil
15ml/1 tbsp fish sauce
15ml/1 tbsp mild curry paste
150ml/¼ pint/⅔ cup canned
  coconut milk
250ml/8fl oz chicken stock
450g/1lb white fish fillet, cut into
  bite-size pieces
225g/8oz raw prawns, peeled
  and deveined
prawn crackers, to serve

For the vegetable platter
1 small cos lettuce, shredded
115g/4oz/2 cups beansprouts
3 spring onions, shredded
½ cucumber, cut in
  matchstick strips

1 Drain the noodles. Cook them in a pan of lightly salted boiling water according to the packet instructions. Cool under running water and leave immersed in water until required.

2 Put the nuts in a mortar and grind them with a pestle. Add the shallots, lemon grass and garlic, and grind the mixture to a paste. Heat the oil in a large wok or pan and fry the paste for 1–2 minutes, or until the nuts begin to brown.

3 Stir the fish sauce and curry paste into the fried paste, then add the coconut milk and chicken stock. Stir well, then bring to simmering point. Simmer for 10 minutes.

4 Add the fish and prawns. Cook for 3–4 minutes, until the prawns have turned pink and the fish is translucent. Remove the seafood with a slotted spoon and arrange it in separate piles on a large platter. Drain the noodles well and heap them on the platter, with the vegetables and prawn crackers in neat piles.

5 Pour the coconut stock into a tureen or earthenware pot and serve with the platter of seafood and vegetables.

Snapper & Tamarind Noodle Soup

Tamarind gives this light, fragrant noodle soup a slightly sour taste. It is available from Asian food stores and there is really no substitute.

Serves 4
2 litres/3½ pints/8 cups water
1 whole red snapper or mullet, about 1kg/2¼ lb, cleaned
1 onion, sliced
50g/2oz tamarind pods
15ml/1 tbsp fish sauce
15ml/1 tbsp sugar
15ml/1 tbsp vegetable oil
2 garlic cloves, finely chopped
2 lemon grass stalks, very finely chopped
4 ripe tomatoes, roughly chopped
30ml/2 tbsp yellow bean paste
225g/8oz rice vermicelli, soaked in warm water until soft
115g/4oz/2 cups beansprouts
8–10 fresh basil or mint sprigs
30ml/2 tbsp roasted peanuts, finely chopped
salt and freshly ground black pepper

1 Bring the measured water to the boil in a large, heavy-based saucepan. Lower the heat and add the fish, with the onion slices and 2.5ml/ ½ tsp salt. Simmer over a low heat until the fish is cooked through.

2 Carefully remove the fish from the stock and set it aside. Add the tamarind, fish sauce and sugar to the stock. Cook for about 5 minutes, then strain the stock into a large jug or bowl. Carefully remove all the bones from the fish, keeping the flesh in big pieces.

3 Heat the oil in a large frying pan. Add the garlic and lemon grass and stir-fry for a few seconds. Stir in the tomatoes and bean paste. Cook gently for 5–7 minutes, until the tomatoes have softened. Add the stock, bring back to a simmer and adjust the seasoning, if necessary.

4 Drain the vermicelli. Plunge it into a saucepan of boiling water for a few minutes, drain and divide among four warmed soup bowls. Add the beansprouts, fish and basil or mint. Top up each bowl with the hot soup and sprinkle the peanuts on top. Serve immediately.

Seafood Soup Noodles

Described as a soup, but very substantial, this would be the ideal choice for a late night, after-theatre supper with friends.

Serves 6
175g/6oz tiger prawns, peeled and deveined
225g/8oz monkfish fillet, cut into chunks
225/8oz salmon fillet, cut into chunks
5ml/1 tsp vegetable oil
15ml/1 tbsp dry white wine
225g/8oz dried egg noodles
1.2 litres/2 pints/5 cups fish stock
1 carrot, thinly sliced
225g/8oz asparagus, cut into 5cm/2in lengths
30ml/2 tbsp dark soy sauce
5ml/1 tsp sesame oil
salt and freshly ground black pepper
2 spring onions, cut into thin rings, to garnish

1 Mix the prawns and fish in a bowl. Add the vegetable oil and wine with 1.5ml/ ¼ tsp salt and a little pepper. Mix lightly, cover and marinate in a cool place for 15 minutes.

2 Bring a large saucepan of water to the boil and cook the noodles for 4 minutes, until just tender, or according to the instructions on the packet. Drain the noodles thoroughly and divide among six serving bowls. Keep hot.

3 Bring the fish stock to the boil in a separate pan. Add the prawns and monkfish, cook for 1 minute, then add the salmon and cook for 2 minutes more.

4 Using a slotted spoon, carefully lift the fish and prawns out of the fish stock, add to the noodles in the bowls and continue to keep hot.

5 Strain the stock through a sieve lined with muslin or cheesecloth into a clean pan. Bring to the boil and cook the carrot and asparagus for 2 minutes, then stir in the soy sauce and sesame oil.

6 Pour the stock and vegetables over the noodles and seafood, garnish with the spring onions and serve immediately.

Noodle Soup with Pork & Pickle

A satisfying and warming soup from western China, a region famous for its delicious spicy pickles.

Serves 4

1 litre/1¾ pints/4 cups
  chicken stock
350g/12oz dried medium
  egg noodles
15ml/1 tbsp dried shrimp,
  soaked in water
15ml/1 tbsp vegetable oil
225g/8oz lean pork,
  finely shredded
15ml/1 tbsp yellow bean paste
15ml/1 tbsp soy sauce
115g/4oz Szechuan hot pickle,
  rinsed, drained and shredded
pinch of granulated sugar
salt and freshly ground
  black pepper
2 spring onions, finely sliced,
  to garnish

1 Bring the chicken stock to the boil in a large saucepan. Add the egg noodles and cook until almost tender. Drain the dried shrimp, rinse under cold running water, drain again and add to the stock. Lower the heat and simmer for 2 minutes. Season to taste. Keep hot.

2 Heat the oil in a frying pan or wok. Add the pork and stir-fry over a high heat for about 3 minutes.

3 Add the yellow bean paste and soy sauce to the pork and stir-fry for 1 minute, then add the hot pickle and sugar. Stir-fry for 1 minute more.

4 Divide the noodles and stock among warmed soup bowls. Spoon the pork mixture on top, then sprinkle with the spring onions and serve at once.

> **Cook's Tip**
> *Available in cans from Chinese food stores, Szechuan hot pickle is based on kohlrabi. It has a very spicy and salty flavour. Other Chinese pickles that could be used include the milder winter pickle, made from salted cabbage or the sour snow pickle, made from salted mustard greens.*

Hanoi Beef & Noodle Soup

Millions of Vietnamese enjoy this fragrant and sustaining soup for breakfast.

Serves 4–6

1 onion
1.5kg/3–3½lb beef shank
  with bones
1 bay leaf
2.5cm/1in piece of fresh
  root ginger
1 star anise
2 whole cloves
2.5ml/½ tsp fennel seeds
1 piece of cassia bark or
  cinnamon stick
3 litres/5 pints/12 cups water
dash of fish sauce
juice of 1 lime
150g/5oz fillet steak
450g/1lb fresh flat rice noodles
salt

For the garnish accompaniments

1 small red onion, sliced into rings
115g/4oz/2 cups beansprouts
2 fresh red chillies, seeded
  and sliced
2 spring onions, finely sliced
a handful of fresh
  coriander leaves
lime wedges

1 Cut the onion in half. Grill under a high heat, cut side up, until the exposed sides are caramelized, and deep brown. Set aside.

2 Cut the meat into large chunks and place with the bones in a large saucepan. Add the caramelized onion, bay leaf, ginger, star anise, cloves, fennel seeds and cassia bark or cinnamon.

3 Pour in the measured water, bring to the boil, then lower the heat and simmer for 2–3 hours, skimming occasionally.

4 Remove the meat from the stock. When cool enough to handle, cut it into small pieces, discarding the bones. Strain the stock and return to the pan with the meat. Bring back to the boil and season with the fish sauce and lime juice.

5 Slice the fillet steak very thinly. Place the garnishes in separate serving bowls. Cook the noodles in a large saucepan of lightly salted boiling water until *al dente*. Drain and divide among warmed bowls. Top with the steak, ladle hot stock over and serve, offering the accompaniments separately.

Pasta, Melon & Prawn Salad

Orange-fleshed cantaloupe or Charentais melon looks spectacular in this salad.

Serves 4–6
175g/6oz/1½ cups dried pasta shapes
1 large melon
225g/8oz cooked peeled prawns
30ml/2 tbsp olive oil
15ml/1 tbsp tarragon vinegar
30ml/2 tbsp snipped fresh chives or chopped parsley
shredded Chinese leaves
fresh herb sprigs, to garnish

1 Bring a large pan of lightly salted water to the boil and cook the pasta until it is *al dente*. Drain, rinse under cold water and drain again. Put it into a bowl and leave until cold.

2 Cut the melon in half and remove the seeds with a teaspoon. Carefully scoop the flesh into balls with a melon baller and add to the pasta, with the prawns.

3 Whisk the oil, vinegar and chopped herbs in a bowl. Pour on to the prawn mixture and turn to coat. Cover and chill for at least 30 minutes.

4 Line a shallow serving bowl with the shredded Chinese leaves, pile the prawn mixture on top and garnish with the herb sprigs. Serve at once.

> **Cook's Tip**
> *For an attractive presentation, serve the salad in the melon shells, lined with the Chinese leaves.*

> **Variation**
> • *For a really special treat, substitute chopped cooked lobster meat for the prawns.*
> • *For a different flavour and texture, use a mixture of Ogen, cantaloupe and watermelon.*

Crab Pasta Salad with Spicy Cocktail Dressing

A variation on a very popular starter, this salad is certain to go down well.

Serves 6
350g/12oz/3 cups dried fusilli
1 small red pepper, seeded and finely chopped
2 x 175g/6oz cans white crab meat, drained
115g/4oz cherry tomatoes, halved
¼ cucumber, halved, seeded and sliced into crescents
15ml/1 tbsp lemon juice
salt and freshly ground black pepper
fresh basil, to garnish

For the dressing
300ml/½ pint/1¼ cups low-fat natural yogurt
2 celery sticks, finely chopped
10ml/2 tsp horseradish cream
2.5ml/½ tsp ground paprika
2.5ml/½ tsp Dijon mustard
30ml/2 tbsp sweet tomato pickle or chutney

1 Bring a large pan of lightly salted water to the boil and cook the pasta until it is *al dente*. Drain, rinse under cold water, and drain again.

2 Put the chopped red pepper in a heatproof bowl and pour over boiling water to cover. Leave to stand for 1 minute, then drain, rinse under cold water and drain again. Pat dry on kitchen paper.

3 Drain the crab meat and pick it over carefully, removing any stray pieces of shell. Put the crab meat into a bowl, and add the tomatoes and cucumber. Season with salt and pepper to taste, then sprinkle with the lemon juice.

4 Make the dressing. Put the yogurt, celery, horseradish cream, paprika, mustard and pickle or chutney into a bowl and mix well. Season with salt, if necessary.

5 Stir in the diced red pepper and the pasta. Transfer the mixture to a serving dish. Spoon the crab mixture on top and mix well. Garnish with fresh basil and serve.

Marinated Chicken & Pasta Salad

This tastes good when the chicken is served warm, but it can be served cold, if that is more convenient.

Serves 6
5ml/1 tsp ground cumin seeds
5ml/1 tsp ground paprika
5ml/1 tsp ground turmeric
1–2 garlic cloves, crushed
45–60ml/3–4 tbsp fresh
   lime juice
4 skinless, boneless
   chicken breasts
225g/8oz/2 cups dried rigatoni
1 red pepper, seeded
   and chopped
2 celery sticks, thinly sliced
1 small onion, finely chopped
6 stuffed green olives, halved
30ml/2 tbsp clear honey
15ml/1 tbsp wholegrain mustard
salt and freshly ground
   black pepper
mixed salad leaves, to serve

1 Mix the cumin, paprika, turmeric, garlic and 30ml/2 tbsp of the lime juice in a bowl. Season to taste with a little salt and pepper. Rub this mixture over the chicken breasts. Lay them in a shallow dish, cover with clear film and leave in a cool place for about 3 hours or overnight.

2 Preheat the oven to 200°C/400°F/Gas 6. Place the chicken breasts in a single layer on a rack set over a roasting tin. Bake for 20 minutes.

3 Meanwhile, bring a large pan of lightly salted water to the boil and cook the rigatoni until al dente. Drain, rinse under cold water and drain again. Leave until cold.

4 Put the red pepper, celery, onion and olives into a large bowl. Add the pasta and mix carefully.

5 Mix the honey, mustard and the remaining lime juice to taste in a jug. Pour the mixture over the pasta. Toss to coat.

6 Cut the chicken into bite-size pieces. Arrange the mixed salad leaves on a serving dish, spoon the pasta mixture into the centre, top with the spicy chicken pieces and serve.

Curried Chicken Salad with Penne

There are several versions of this popular salad. This one has a dressing based on low-fat yogurt, so it is a relatively healthy option.

Serves 4
2 cooked boneless, skinless
   chicken breasts
175g/6oz French beans, trimmed
   and cut in short lengths
350g/12oz/3 cups dried penne,
   preferably mixed colours
150ml/¼ pint/⅔ cup
   low-fat yogurt
5ml/1 tsp mild curry powder
1 garlic clove, crushed
1 fresh green chilli, seeded and
   finely chopped
30ml/2 tbsp chopped
   fresh coriander
4 firm ripe tomatoes, peeled,
   seeded and cut in strips
salt and freshly ground
   black pepper
fresh coriander leaves, to garnish

1 Cut the chicken breasts into bite-size pieces. Bring a large pan of lightly salted water to the boil and cook the French beans for 2–3 minutes. Lift them into a colander, using a slotted spoon, and drain under cold water. Drain again.

2 Bring the water back to the boil and cook the pasta until it is al dente. Drain, rinse under cold water and drain again.

3 Mix the yogurt, curry powder, garlic, chilli and chopped coriander together in a bowl. Stir in the chicken pieces and leave to stand for 30 minutes.

4 Put the pasta in a glass bowl, and toss with the beans and tomatoes. Spoon over the chicken and sauce. Garnish with coriander leaves and serve.

Variation
For an alternative dressing, mix together 150ml/¼ pint/⅔ cup mayonnaise, 10ml/2 tsp concentrated curry sauce, 2.5ml/½ tsp lemon juice and 10ml/2 tsp sieved apricot jam. Add the chicken to the dressing and chill in the fridge for 30 minutes before mixing with the pasta and serving.

Duck & Rigatoni Salad

This sophisticated salad has a delicious sweet-sour dressing which goes wonderfully well with the richness of duck.

Serves 6
2 duck breasts, boned
5ml/1 tsp coriander
  seeds, crushed
350g/12oz/3 cups rigatoni
150ml/ 1/4 pint/ 2/3 cup fresh
  orange juice
15ml/1 tbsp lemon juice
10ml/2 tsp clear honey
1 shallot, finely chopped
1 garlic clove, crushed
1 celery stick, chopped
75g/3oz dried cherries
45ml/3 tbsp port
15ml/1 tbsp chopped fresh mint,
  plus extra to garnish
30ml/2 tbsp chopped fresh
  coriander, plus extra to garnish
1 eating apple, diced
2 oranges, segmented
salt and freshly ground
  black pepper

1 Preheat the grill. Remove the skin and fat from the duck breasts, and season them with salt and pepper. Rub them with the crushed coriander seeds. Place them on a grill rack and grill for 7–10 minutes. Wrap them in foil and leave for 20 minutes.

2 Bring a large pan of lightly salted water to the boil and cook the pasta until it is *al dente*. Drain, rinse under cold water and drain again. Leave to cool.

3 Put the orange juice, lemon juice, honey, shallot, garlic, celery, cherries, port, mint and fresh coriander into a bowl, whisk together and leave the dressing to stand for 30 minutes.

4 Slice the duck very thinly. (It should be pink in the centre.) Put the pasta into a bowl, add the dressing, apple and oranges. Toss well. Transfer the salad to a serving plate. Add the duck slices, and garnish with the extra coriander and mint.

> **Cook's Tip**
> If you do not like your duck pink in the middle, then grill it for a little longer.

Devilled Ham & Pineapple Penne Salad

Ham and pineapple are often paired. In this salad, the combination works particularly well, thanks to the fruity dressing.

Serves 4
225g/8oz/2 cups
  wholewheat penne
150ml/ 1/4 pint/ 2/3 cup low-fat
  natural yogurt
15ml/1 tbsp cider vinegar
5ml/1 tsp wholegrain mustard
a large pinch of caster sugar
30ml/2 tbsp hot mango chutney
115g/4oz cooked ham, diced
200g/7oz can natural pineapple
  chunks, drained
2 celery sticks, chopped
1/2 green pepper, seeded
  and diced
15ml/1 tbsp flaked toasted
  almonds, roughly chopped
salt and freshly ground
  black pepper

1 Bring a large pan of lightly salted water to the boil and cook the pasta until it is *al dente*. Drain, rinse under cold water and drain again. Leave to cool.

2 Mix the yogurt, vinegar, mustard, sugar and mango chutney in a large bowl. Add the pasta, and season with salt and pepper to taste. Toss lightly together.

3 Pile the dressed pasta on to a serving dish. Scatter over the ham, pineapple, celery and green pepper.

4 Sprinkle the toasted almonds on top. Serve at once.

> **Variations**
> • Substitute garlic croûtons for the toasted almonds to garnish the salad.
> • Instead of pineapple chunks, you could use chopped fresh or canned mangoes.
> • Add a diced green eating apple with the celery and green pepper in step 3.

Bacon & Bean Pasta Salad

This tasty pasta salad is subtly flavoured with smoked bacon in a light, flavoursome dressing.

Serves 4

225g/8oz green beans
350g/12oz/3 cups dried
   wholewheat fusilli or spirali
8 rindless lean smoked back
   bacon rashers
350g/12oz cherry
   tomatoes, halved
2 bunches of spring
   onions, chopped
400g/14oz can chick-peas, rinsed
   and drained
90ml/6 tbsp tomato juice
30ml/2 tbsp balsamic vinegar
5ml/1 tsp ground cumin
5ml/1 tsp ground coriander
30ml/2 tbsp chopped
   fresh coriander
salt and freshly ground
   black pepper

1 Bring a large pan of lightly salted water to the boil and cook the beans for 3–4 minutes, until crisp-tender. Lift them out with a slotted spoon and place in a colander. Refresh under cold water and drain.

2 Bring the water back to the boil, add the pasta and cook until *al dente*.

3 Meanwhile, grill the bacon until crisp. Dice or crumble it and add it to the beans.

4 Mix the tomatoes, spring onions and chick-peas in a large bowl. In a jug, mix together the tomato juice, vinegar, cumin, ground coriander and fresh coriander, and season to taste with salt and pepper. Pour the dressing over the tomato mixture.

5 Drain the pasta thoroughly and add it to the tomato mixture with the beans and bacon. Toss well. Serve warm or cold.

> **Variation**
> You could substitute canned haricot beans or flageolets for the chick-peas.

Herbed Beef & Pasta Salad

Fillet of beef is such a luxury cut that it makes sense to stretch it if you can. Serving it as part of a pasta salad is an excellent way of doing this.

Serves 6

450g/1lb beef fillet
450g/1lb fresh tagliatelle
   with herbs
1/2 cucumber
115g/4oz cherry tomatoes, halved

For the marinade

15ml/1 tbsp soy sauce
15ml/1 tbsp sherry
5ml/1 tsp fresh root ginger, grated
1 garlic clove, crushed

For the herb dressing

30–45ml/2–3 tbsp
   horseradish sauce
150ml/ 1/4 pint/ 2/3 cup low-fat
   natural yogurt
1 garlic clove, crushed
30–45ml/2–3 tbsp chopped
   fresh herbs
salt and freshly ground
   black pepper

1 Mix all the marinade ingredients in a shallow dish, add the beef and turn it over to coat it. Cover with clear film and leave for 30 minutes to allow the flavours to penetrate the meat.

2 Preheat the grill. Lift the fillet out of the marinade and pat it dry with kitchen paper. Place it on a grill rack and grill for 8 minutes on each side, basting with the marinade during cooking, then put it on a plate, cover with foil and leave to stand for 20 minutes.

3 Bring a pan of lightly salted water to the boil, add the pasta and cook until it is *al dente*. Drain, rinse under cold water and drain again.

4 Cut the cucumber in half lengthways, scoop out the seeds with a teaspoon and slice the flesh thinly into crescents.

5 Mix all the dressing ingredients in a large bowl. Add the pasta, cucumber and cherry tomatoes, and toss to coat. Divide among six plates. Slice the beef thinly and fan out the slices alongside the salad. Serve immediately.

Potato & Cellophane Noodle Salad

Oriental noodles aren't the obvious choice for salads in the West, but perhaps they should be, as they add a new dimension.

Serves 4

2 medium potatoes, peeled and
    cut into eighths
175g/6oz cellophane noodles,
    soaked in hot water until soft
30ml/2 tbsp vegetable oil
1 onion, finely sliced
5ml/1 tsp ground turmeric
60ml/4 tbsp gram flour
5ml/1 tsp grated lemon rind
60–75ml/4–5 tbsp lemon juice
45ml/3 tbsp Thai fish sauce
4 spring onions, finely sliced
salt and freshly ground black
    pepper (optional)

1 Place the potatoes in a saucepan. Add lightly salted water to cover, bring to the boil and cook for about 15 minutes, until tender but not soggy. Drain and set aside to cool.

2 Meanwhile, bring a second pan of lightly salted water to the boil. Drain the soaked noodles, add them to the water and cook briefly, until they are just tender. Drain, rinse under cold running water and drain again.

3 Heat the oil in a frying pan and fry the onion with the turmeric for about 5 minutes, until golden brown. Drain the onion, reserving the oil.

4 Heat a small frying pan. Add the gram flour and stir constantly for about 4 minutes until it turns light golden brown.

5 Mix the drained potatoes, noodles and fried onion in a large bowl. Add the reserved oil and the toasted gram flour with the lemon rind and juice, fish sauce and spring onions. Mix together well and adjust the seasoning if necessary. Serve at once.

Cook's Tip
Cellophane noodles need very little cooking and will probably be ready in 1–2 minutes. Check the instructions on the packet.

Buckwheat Noodles with Smoked Salmon

The slightly earthy flavour of buckwheat noodles complements the smoked salmon perfectly in this warm salad.

Serves 4

225g/8oz buckwheat or
    soba noodles
15ml/1 tbsp oyster sauce
juice of ½ lemon
30ml/2 tbsp light olive oil
115g/4oz smoked salmon, cut
    into thin strips
115g/4oz/2 cups young
    pea sprouts
2 ripe tomatoes, peeled, seeded
    and cut into strips
15ml/1 tbsp snipped chives
salt and freshly ground
    black pepper

1 Bring a large pan of lightly salted water to the boil and cook the noodles until just tender, checking the packet for instructions on timing. Drain, rinse under cold water and drain again.

2 Tip the noodles into a large bowl. Add the oyster sauce and lemon juice, and season with pepper to taste. Moisten with the olive oil.

3 Add the smoked salmon, pea sprouts, tomatoes and chives. Mix well and serve at once.

Variations
• *Young pea sprouts are only available for a short time. You can substitute watercress, young leeks or your favourite green vegetable or herb.*
• *This recipe would also be delicious made with buckling or smoked eel instead of salmon.*

Sesame Duck & Noodle Salad

The marinade for this main-course salad is a marvellous blend of spices.

Serves 4
2 duck breasts, thinly sliced
15ml/1 tbsp oil
225g/8oz medium dried
  egg noodles
150g/5oz sugar snap peas
2 carrots, cut into 7.5cm/
  3in sticks
6 spring onions, sliced
salt
30ml/2 tbsp fresh coriander
  leaves, to garnish

For the marinade
15ml/1 tbsp sesame oil
5ml/1 tsp ground coriander
5ml/1 tsp Chinese five-
  spice powder

For the dressing
15ml/1 tbsp garlic vinegar or
  balsamic vinegar
5ml/1 tsp soft light brown sugar
5ml/1 tsp soy sauce
15ml/1 tbsp toasted
  sesame seeds
30ml/2 tbsp sunflower oil
15ml/1 tbsp sesame oil
ground black pepper

1 Place the duck in a shallow dish. Mix all the ingredients for the marinade. Pour the mixture over the duck and use your hands to rub in the mixture. Cover and set aside for 30 minutes.

2 Heat the oil in a frying pan, add the slices of duck breast and stir-fry them for 3–4 minutes until cooked. Set aside.

3 Bring a saucepan of lightly salted water to the boil. Add the noodles, place the sugar snap peas and carrots in a steamer on top and cook for the time suggested on the noodle packet. Set the vegetables aside. Drain the noodles, refresh them under cold running water and drain again. Tip them into a large serving bowl.

4 Make the dressing. Mix the vinegar, sugar, soy sauce and toasted sesame seeds. Season with ground black pepper and whisk in the oils.

5 Pour the dressing over the noodles and mix well. Add the sugar snap peas, carrots, spring onions and duck slices, and toss to mix. Scatter the coriander leaves over and serve.

Curry Fried Pork & Noodle Salad

This popular salad combines an interesting variety of flavours and textures.

Serves 4
225g/8oz pork fillet, trimmed
2 garlic cloves, finely chopped
2 slices of fresh root ginger,
  finely chopped
30–45ml/2–3 tbsp rice wine
15ml/1 tbsp vegetable oil
2 lemon grass stalks,
  finely chopped
10ml/2 tsp curry powder
175g/6oz/3 cups beansprouts

225g/8oz rice vermicelli, soaked
  in warm water until soft
1/2 lettuce, finely shredded
30ml/2 tbsp fresh mint leaves
lemon juice
Thai fish sauce
salt and freshly ground
  black pepper

To garnish
2 spring onions, chopped
25g/1oz/1/4 cup roasted
  peanuts, chopped
pork crackling (optional)

1 Cut the pork into thin strips. Place these in a shallow dish with half the garlic and ginger. Season with salt and pepper, pour over 30ml/2 tbsp of the rice wine, stir and marinate for 1 hour.

2 Heat the oil in a frying pan. Add the remaining garlic and ginger, and fry for a few seconds until fragrant. Stir in the pork, with the marinade, and add the lemon grass and curry powder. Fry until the pork is golden and cooked through, adding more rice wine if the mixture seems too dry.

3 Meanwhile, blanch the beansprouts in boiling water for 1 minute. Drain, refresh under cold water and drain again.

4 Using the same water, cook the drained rice vermicelli for 3–5 minutes, until tender. Drain and rinse under cold running water. Drain well and tip into a bowl.

5 Add the beansprouts, shredded lettuce and mint to the bowl. Season with lemon juice and fish sauce to taste. Toss lightly. Divide the noodle mixture among individual plates. Arrange the pork mixture on top. Garnish with spring onions, roasted peanuts and pork crackling, if using.

FISH & SEAFOOD

Tuna & Mixed Vegetable Pasta
Conchiglie with Tomato & Tuna Sauce
Pasta with Tuna, Capers & Anchovies
Salmon Pasta with Parsley Sauce
Spaghetti with Hot-&-Sour Fish
Tagliatelle with Cucumber & Smoked Salmon
Fusilli with Smoked Trout
Smoked Trout Cannelloni
Penne with Salmon & Dill
Tagliatelle with Smoked Trout & Dill
Spaghetti with Salmon & Prawns
Linguine with Smoked Salmon & Mushrooms
Smoked Haddock in Parsley Sauce
Hot Spicy Prawns with Campanelle
Mixed Summer Pasta
Saffron & Seafood Pappardelle
Seafood Conchiglione with Spinach
Baked Seafood Pasta
Pasta with Scallops in Warm Green Tartare Sauce
Devilled Crab Conchiglione
Spaghetti with White Clam Sauce
Black Pasta with Raw Vegetables
Trenette with Shellfish
Tagliolini with Mussels & Clams
Spaghetti Marinara
Baked Seafood Spaghetti
Spaghetti with Clams
Linguine with Clam & Tomato Sauce
Soba Noodles with Nori
Egg Noodles with Tuna & Tomato Sauce
Seafood & Vermicelli Stir-fry
Buckwheat Noodles with Smoked Trout
Noodles with Prawns in Lemon Sauce
Chilli Squid & Noodles
Sweet & Sour Prawns with Noodles
Spicy Singapore Noodles

Tuna & Mixed Vegetable Pasta

Mushrooms, tuna and pasta make a tasty combination, and the fat content is satisfyingly low.

Serves 4
15ml/1 tbsp olive oil
175g/6oz/2 cups sliced
   button mushrooms
1 garlic clove, crushed
½ red pepper, seeded
   and chopped
15ml/1 tbsp tomato purée

300ml/½ pint/1¼ cups
   tomato juice
115g/4oz/1 cup frozen peas
15–30ml/1–2 tbsp drained
   pickled green
   peppercorns, crushed
275g/10oz/2½ cups wholewheat
   pasta shapes
200g/7oz can tuna chunks in
   brine, drained
6 spring onions, diagonally sliced
salt

1 Heat the olive oil in a heavy-based saucepan. Add the mushrooms, garlic and red pepper, and sauté gently over a low heat until softened.

2 Stir in the tomato purée, then add the tomato juice, peas and some or all of the crushed peppercorns, depending on how spicy you would like the sauce. Bring to the boil, lower the heat and simmer.

3 Bring a large pan of lightly salted water to the boil and cook the pasta until *al dente*.

4 When the pasta is almost ready, add the tuna to the sauce and heat through gently. Stir in the spring onions. Drain the pasta, tip it into a heated bowl and pour over the sauce. Serve at once.

> **Variations**
> • Substitute 115g/4oz/⅔ cup frozen or canned sweetcorn kernels for the peas.
> • Use canned or flaked smoked mackerel fillets instead of the canned tuna.

Conchiglie with Tomato & Tuna Sauce

The trick with low-fat food is to make it as flavoursome as you can, using aromatics, herbs and extra flavourings such as capers.

Serves 6
1 medium onion, finely chopped
1 celery stick, finely chopped
1 red pepper, seeded and diced
1 garlic clove, crushed
150ml/¼ pint/⅔ cup
   vegetable stock
400g/14oz can
   chopped tomatoes

15ml/1 tbsp tomato purée
10ml/2 tsp caster sugar
15ml/1 tbsp chopped
   fresh basil
15ml/1 tbsp chopped
   fresh parsley
450g/1lb/4 cups dried conchiglie
400g/14oz can tuna in
   brine, drained
30ml/2 tbsp bottled capers in
   vinegar, drained
salt and freshly ground
   black pepper

1 Put the onion, celery, red pepper and garlic into a large non-stick pan. Add the vegetable stock, bring to the boil and cook over a medium heat for about 5 minutes, or until most of the stock has evaporated and very little liquid remains.

2 Stir in the tomatoes, tomato purée, sugar, basil and parsley. Season to taste with salt and pepper, and bring to the boil over a medium heat.

3 Lower the heat and simmer the sauce for 30 minutes until thickened, stirring occasionally.

4 Meanwhile, bring a large pan of lightly salted water to the boil and cook the pasta until *al dente*. Drain thoroughly and transfer to a warm serving dish.

5 Flake the tuna into large chunks and add it to the sauce with the capers. Heat gently, stirring occasionally but without breaking up the fish, for 1–2 minutes. Pour over the pasta, toss gently and serve at once.

Pasta with Tuna, Capers & Anchovies

This piquant sauce could be made without tomatoes – just heat the oil, add the other ingredients and heat through gently before tossing with the pasta.

Serves 4
15ml/1 tbsp olive oil
2 garlic cloves, crushed
2 x 400g/14oz cans
  chopped tomatoes
400g/14oz can tuna in
  brine, drained
6 drained canned anchovy fillets
30ml/2 tbsp drained bottled
  capers in vinegar
30ml/2 tbsp chopped fresh basil
450g/1lb/4 cups dried rigatoni,
  penne or garganelli
salt and freshly ground
  black pepper
fresh basil sprigs, to garnish

1 Heat the olive oil in a heavy-based saucepan. Add the garlic and cook over a medium heat until golden, but not browned. Lower the heat, stir in the tomatoes and simmer for about 25 minutes, until thickened.

2 Flake the tuna and cut the anchovies in half. Stir the fish into the sauce with the capers and chopped basil. Season well with salt and pepper.

3 Bring a large pan of lightly salted water to the boil and cook the pasta until it is *al dente*.

4 Drain the pasta well, return to the clean pan and toss with the sauce. Serve immediately in warmed bowls, garnished with the fresh basil sprigs.

Cook's Tip
Olive oil is high in monounsaturated fats and so is a healthy choice. However, if you want to cut the fat content of this dish still further, omit it and coat the base of the pan very thinly with light spray oil.

Salmon Pasta with Parsley Sauce

Delicately flavoured and with a lovely colour, salmon makes a surprisingly substantial meal, especially when tossed with pasta shapes.

Serves 4
450g/1lb salmon fillet, skinned
150g/5oz/²⁄₃ cup very low-fat
  fromage frais
45ml/3 tbsp finely
  chopped parsley
finely grated rind of ¹⁄₂ orange
225g/8oz/2 cups dried penne
  or spirali
175g/6oz cherry tomatoes, halved
salt and freshly ground
  black pepper

1 Cut the salmon into bite-size pieces, arrange on a heatproof plate and cover with foil. Mix the fromage frais, parsley and orange rind in a bowl, and stir in pepper to taste.

2 Bring a large pan of lightly salted water to the boil, add the pasta and return to the boil. Lower the heat, place the plate of salmon on top and simmer for 10–12 minutes, or until both the pasta and salmon are cooked.

3 Lift off the plate of salmon and drain the pasta well. Put the pasta in a bowl and toss with the fromage frais mixture until coated. Add the tomatoes and salmon, and toss again, taking care not to break up the fish too much. Serve hot or cold.

Cook's Tip
Salmon is an oily fish and contains 8–12 per cent fat, mostly in the form of Omega 3 fatty acids, which are believed to be beneficial in helping to prevent coronary heart disease. In this recipe, the fat content of the fish is counterbalanced by using very low-fat or even virtually fat-free fromage frais.

Spaghetti with Hot-&-Sour Fish

Hoi-sin sauce is the secret ingredient that makes this taste so good.

Serves 4

15ml/1 tbsp olive oil
1 large onion, chopped
5ml/1 tsp ground turmeric
1 fresh green chilli, cored, seeded and finely chopped
225g/8oz courgettes, thinly sliced
115g/4oz/1 cup shelled peas, thawed if frozen
350g/12oz dried spaghetti
450g/1lb monkfish tail, skinned and cut into bite-size pieces
10ml/2 tsp lemon juice
75ml/5 tbsp hoi–sin sauce
150ml/¼ pint/⅔ cup water
salt and freshly ground black pepper
a sprig of fresh dill, to garnish

1 Heat the oil in a large frying pan and fry the onion for 5 minutes, until softened. Stir in the turmeric and cook for 1 minute more.

2 Add the chilli, courgettes and peas, and fry over a low heat until the vegetables have softened.

3 Meanwhile, bring a large saucepan of lightly salted water to the boil, add the spaghetti and cook until it is *al dente*.

4 Stir the fish, lemon juice, hoi-sin sauce and water into the vegetable mixture. Bring to the boil, then lower the heat and simmer for 5 minutes, or until the fish is tender. Season to taste with salt and pepper.

5 Drain the spaghetti thoroughly and tip it into a serving bowl. Add the sauce and toss to coat. Serve immediately, garnished with a sprig of fresh dill.

Cook's Tip
Monkfish tail is quite often skinned before the shop displays it for sale. Nevertheless, it is still essential to strip off the transparent membrane surrounding the flesh, as this will become tough on cooking.

Tagliatelle with Cucumber & Smoked Salmon

The light texture of the cucumber complements the fish perfectly in this summery dish.

Serves 4

½ cucumber
350g/12oz dried tagliatelle
25g/1oz/2 tbsp butter
grated rind of 1 orange
30ml/2 tbsp chopped fresh dill
300ml/½ pint/1¼ cups low-fat crème fraîche
15ml/1 tbsp freshly squeezed orange juice
115g/4oz smoked salmon, skinned and cut into thin strips
salt and freshly ground black pepper

1 Cut the cucumber in half lengthways, then, using a small spoon, scoop out and discard the seeds from the centre. Slice the cucumber thinly.

2 Bring a large pan of lightly salted water to the boil, add the tagliatelle and cook until *al dente*.

3 Melt the butter in a heavy-based saucepan and stir in the orange rind and dill. Add the cucumber and cook over a low heat, stirring occasionally, for about 2 minutes.

4 Pour in the low-fat crème fraîche and orange juice, season with salt and pepper to taste and simmer for 1 minute, then stir in the salmon and heat through.

5 Drain the pasta, return it to the pan and add the sauce. Toss lightly to coat. Serve immediately.

Cook's Tip
An economical way to make this sauce is to use smoked salmon offcuts, available from most supermarkets and delicatessens, as they are much cheaper than slices. Smoked trout is also a less expensive alternative.

Fusilli with Smoked Trout

Curly strands of fusilli in a sauce that tastes deceptively creamy are topped with crisp-tender vegetables and smoked fish to make a dish that tastes every bit as good as it looks.

Serves 4–6

2 carrots, cut into
   matchstick strips
1 leek, cut into matchstick strips
2 celery sticks, cut into
   matchstick strips
150ml/ 1/4 pint/ 2/3 cup
   vegetable stock
225g/8oz smoked trout fillets,
   skinned and cut into strips
200g/7oz/scant 1 cup low-fat
   cream cheese
150ml/ 1/4 pint/ 2/3 cup medium
   sweet white wine or fish stock
15ml/1 tbsp chopped fresh dill
   or fennel
225g/8oz dried fusilli lunghi
salt and freshly ground
   black pepper
fresh dill sprigs, to garnish

1 Put the carrots, leek and celery into a pan. Pour in the vegetable stock. Bring to the boil and cook over a high heat for 4–5 minutes, until the vegetables are tender and most of the stock has evaporated. Remove the pan from the heat and add the smoked trout.

2 To make the sauce, put the cream cheese and white wine or fish stock into a large pan, and whisk over a low heat until smooth. Season to taste with salt and pepper. Add the chopped dill or fennel.

3 Bring a large pan of lightly salted water to the boil and cook the pasta until *al dente*.

4 Drain the pasta well and add it to the pan with the sauce. Toss lightly, then transfer to a warmed serving bowl. Top with the cooked vegetables and trout. Serve immediately, garnished with dill sprigs.

> **Variation**
> *Use smoked monkfish instead of trout.*

Smoked Trout Cannelloni

Simmering vegetables in stock instead of frying them in fat or oil produces tasty, moist results.

Serves 4–6

1 large onion, finely chopped
1 garlic clove, crushed
60ml/4 tbsp vegetable stock
2 x 400g/14oz cans
   chopped tomatoes
2.5ml/ 1/2 tsp dried mixed herbs
1 smoked trout, about 400g/14oz
75g/3oz/ 3/4 cup frozen
   peas, thawed
75g/3oz/1 1/2 cups fresh
   white breadcrumbs
16 cannelloni tubes
salt and freshly ground
   black pepper

For the cheese sauce
25g/1oz/2 tbsp low-fat spread
25g/1oz/ 1/4 cup plain flour
350ml/12fl oz/1 1/2 cups
   skimmed milk
freshly grated nutmeg
45ml/3 tbsp freshly grated
   Parmesan cheese

1 Put the onion, garlic and stock in a large pan. Cover and cook for 3 minutes. Remove the lid and continue to cook, stirring occasionally, until the stock has reduced entirely. Stir in the tomatoes and dried herbs. Simmer, uncovered, for 10 minutes more, or until very thick.

2 Meanwhile, skin the fish, flake the flesh and discard the bones. Put the fish in a bowl and stir in the tomato mixture, peas and breadcrumbs, and season to taste. Leave to cool slightly.

3 Preheat the oven to 190°C/375°F/Gas 5. Spoon the filling into the cannelloni tubes and arrange them in a single layer in an ovenproof dish.

4 Make the sauce. Put the low-fat spread, flour and milk into a pan and cook over a medium heat, whisking constantly until the sauce thickens. Simmer for 2–3 minutes, stirring all the time. Season to taste with salt, pepper and nutmeg.

5 Pour the sauce over the cannelloni and sprinkle with the Parmesan. Bake for 35–40 minutes, or until the top is golden and bubbling. Leave to stand for 5–10 minutes before serving.

Penne with Salmon & Dill

Rosé wine accentuates the colour of the salmon and gives this simple dish a hint of sophistication.

Serves 6
350g/12oz fresh salmon
    fillet, skinned
115g/4oz sliced smoked salmon
350g/12oz/3 cups dried penne
1–2 shallots, finely chopped

115g/4oz/1½ cups button
    mushrooms, quartered
150ml/¼ pint/⅔ cup rosé wine
150ml/¼ pint/⅔ cup fish stock
150ml/¼ pint/⅔ cup low-fat
    crème fraîche
30ml/2 tbsp chopped fresh dill
salt and freshly ground
    black pepper
fresh dill sprigs, to garnish

1 Cut the fresh salmon into 2.5cm/1in cubes. Cut the smoked salmon into 1cm/½in strips and set aside.

2 Bring a large pan of lightly salted water to the boil and cook the pasta until it is *al dente*.

3 Meanwhile, put the shallots and mushrooms into a non-stick pan and pour in the rosé wine. Bring to the boil over a medium heat and cook for about 5 minutes, or until the wine has reduced almost completely.

4 Pour in the fish stock and crème fraîche, and stir until smooth. Add the fresh salmon, cover the pan and simmer gently over a low heat for 2–3 minutes, or until the salmon is cooked.

5 Drain the pasta and tip it into a warmed serving dish. Add the smoked salmon and dill to the sauce, season to taste with salt and pepper, and pour over the pasta. Toss lightly to mix. Serve at once, garnished with the dill sprigs.

> **Variation**
> *Use fresh and smoked trout instead of the salmon. Substitute red wine for the rosé, as trout does not have the same delicate pink colouring as salmon.*

Tagliatelle with Smoked Trout & Dill

This light pasta dish can also be made with canned tuna or salmon in brine as a store-cupboard alternative for a midweek supper.

Serves 4
350g/12oz fresh or
    dried tagliatelle
275g/10oz smoked trout fillet,
    skinned and flaked
225g/8oz cherry tomatoes, halved
150g/5oz/⅔ cup low-fat fromage
    frais or low-fat natural yogurt
30ml/2 tbsp chopped fresh dill
30ml/2 tbsp chopped fresh chives
salt and freshly ground
    black pepper

1 Bring a large pan of lightly salted water to the boil and cook the pasta until *al dente*. Drain well and return to the clean pan.

2 Toss the flaked trout into the hot pasta, and add the tomatoes and fromage frais or yogurt.

3 Heat gently, without boiling, then stir in the herbs and season with black pepper to taste. Spoon into warmed bowls and serve immediately.

> **Cook's Tip**
> *Low-fat fromage frais can frequently be used in place of cream in sauces, so consider this low-fat option in other recipes too.*

> **Variation**
> *Substitute pappardelle for the tagliatelle and smoked mackerel for the smoked trout. Omit the cherry tomatoes and add strips of red pepper instead. Toss the dressed pasta with finely diced cucumber rather than dill.*

Spaghetti with Salmon & Prawns

Light and fresh-tasting, this is perfect for an *al fresco* meal in summer. Serve with warm ciabatta.

Serves 4
300g/11oz salmon fillet
200ml/7fl oz/scant 1 cup dry
   white wine
a few fresh basil sprigs, plus extra
   basil leaves, to garnish

6 ripe Italian plum tomatoes,
   peeled and finely chopped
150ml/1/4 pint/2/3 cup very low-
   fat fromage frais
350g/12oz fresh or
   dried spaghetti
115g/4oz cooked peeled prawns,
   thawed if frozen
salt and freshly ground
   black pepper

1 Put the salmon skin side up in a wide shallow pan. Pour over the wine, then add the basil sprigs. Sprinkle the fish with salt and pepper. Bring to the boil, cover and simmer gently for no more than 5 minutes. Using a fish slice, lift the fish out of the pan and set it aside to cool a little.

2 Stir the tomatoes and fromage frais into the liquid remaining in the pan and heat gently, without letting the sauce approach boiling point. Meanwhile, bring a large pan of lightly salted water to the boil. Add the pasta and cook until *al dente*.

3 Flake the fish into large chunks, discarding the skin and any bones. Add the fish to the sauce with the prawns, shaking the pan until they are well coated. Taste for seasoning.

4 Drain the pasta and tip it into a warmed bowl. Pour the sauce over the pasta and toss to combine. Serve immediately, garnished with the fresh basil leaves.

> **Cook's Tip**
> *Check the salmon fillet carefully for small bones when you are flaking the flesh. Although the salmon is already filleted, you will always find a few stray "pin" bones. Pick them out carefully, using tweezers or your fingertips.*

Linguine with Smoked Salmon & Mushrooms

Proof positive that pasta dishes need not be high in fat, even when their sauces seem very creamy.

Serves 6
30ml/2 tbsp olive oil
115g/4oz/1 1/4 cups button
   mushrooms, thinly sliced
250ml/8fl oz/1 cup dry
   white wine
7.5ml/1 1/2 tsp fresh dill or 5ml/
   1 tsp dried dill weed

handful of fresh chives, snipped
300ml/1/2 pint/1 1/4 cups very
   low-fat fromage frais
225g/8oz smoked salmon, cut
   into thin strips
lemon juice
350g/12oz fresh linguine
   or spaghetti
salt and freshly ground
   black pepper
whole fresh chives, to garnish

1 Heat the oil in a wide, shallow saucepan. Add the mushrooms and fry over a gentle heat for 4–5 minutes, until they have softened but not coloured.

2 Pour the white wine into the pan. Increase the heat and boil rapidly for about 5 minutes, until the wine has reduced.

3 Stir in the herbs and fromage frais. Fold in the salmon and reheat gently. Stir in pepper and lemon juice to taste. Cover the pan and keep the sauce warm.

4 Bring a large saucepan of lightly salted water to the boil, add the pasta and cook until it is *al dente*. Drain, rinse thoroughly in boiling water and drain again. Turn into a warmed serving dish. Toss gently with the salmon sauce. Serve in warmed bowls, garnished with chives.

> **Cook's Tip**
> *After you have added the fromage frais to the sauce, do not allow it boil or it will curdle.*

Smoked Haddock in Parsley Sauce

Perfect for a family supper, this would be lovely with roasted tomatoes.

Serves 4
450g/1lb smoked haddock fillet
1 small leek or onion, thickly sliced
300ml/ 1/2 pint/1 1/4 cups skimmed milk
1 bouquet garni (bay leaf, thyme and parsley stalks)
225g/8oz/2 cups dried conchiglie
25g/1oz/2 tbsp low-fat spread
25g/1oz/ 1/4 cup plain flour
30ml/2 tbsp chopped fresh parsley
salt and freshly ground black pepper
toasted flaked almonds, to serve (optional)

1 Remove the skin and any bones from the haddock. Put it into a pan with the leek or onion, milk and bouquet garni. Bring to simmering point, cover and cook gently for 8–10 minutes, until the fish flakes easily when tested with the tip of a sharp knife.

2 Strain, reserving the cooking liquid, and discard the bouquet garni. Flake the fish and set it aside with the leek or onion.

3 Bring a large pan of lightly salted water to the boil and cook the pasta until it is *al dente*.

4 Meanwhile, put the low-fat spread and flour in a pan. Whisk in the milk used for cooking the fish. Bring to the boil over a low heat, whisking until smooth. Season with salt and pepper to taste, and add the flaked fish and leek or onion.

5 Drain the pasta thoroughly and tip it into a warmed serving bowl. Add the sauce and chopped parsley. Toss well. Serve at once. Scatter with toasted almonds, if you like.

> **Cook's Tip**
> Skin frozen fish when it is only partially thawed. Slide the tip of a knife under the skin to loosen, grip it firmly and pull it off.

Hot Spicy Prawns with Campanelle

Marinated prawns and grilled turkey rashers make this pasta dish a treat that's hard to beat.

Serves 4–6
225g/8oz cooked tiger prawns, peeled
1–2 garlic cloves, crushed
finely grated rind of 1 lemon
15ml/1 tbsp lemon juice
1.5ml/ 1/4 tsp red chilli paste or a large pinch of dried ground chilli
15ml/1 tbsp light soy sauce
150g/5oz smoked turkey rashers
225g/8oz dried campanelle
2 shallots, finely chopped
90ml/6 tbsp white wine
60ml/4 tbsp fish stock
4 firm ripe tomatoes, peeled, seeded and chopped
30ml/2 tbsp chopped fresh parsley
salt and freshly ground black pepper

1 In a non-metallic bowl, mix the prawns with the garlic, lemon rind and juice, chilli paste or ground chilli and soy sauce. Season to taste with salt and pepper, cover and set aside to marinate for at least 1 hour.

2 Meanwhile, grill the turkey rashers under a preheated moderate grill for about 3–4 minutes. Drain them on kitchen paper, then dice them.

3 Bring a large pan of lightly salted water to the boil and cook the pasta until *al dente*.

4 Meanwhile, put the shallots and wine in a large pan and bring to the boil over a medium heat, then simmer until the shallots are soft and only about half of the wine remains.

5 Add the prawns, together with their marinade, and bring to the boil over a high heat. Stir in the smoked turkey and fish stock. Heat through for 1 minute.

6 Drain the pasta and add it to the pan with the chopped tomatoes and parsley. Toss thoroughly, transfer to a warmed bowl and serve immediately.

Saffron & Seafood Pappardelle

This resembles a Breton fish stew, and the broad ribbons of tender pasta make a welcome bonus.

Serves 4
a large pinch of saffron strands
4 sun-dried tomatoes, chopped
5ml/1 tsp fresh thyme
60ml/4 tbsp hot water
225g/8oz baby squid
225g/8oz monkfish fillet
2–3 garlic cloves, crushed
2 small onions, quartered
1 small fennel bulb, trimmed
    and sliced
150ml/ 1/4 pint/ 2/3 cup
    white wine
12 large raw prawns in
    their shells
225g/8oz fresh pappardelle
salt and freshly ground
    black pepper
30ml/2 tbsp chopped fresh
    parsley, to garnish

1 Put the saffron, sun-dried tomatoes and thyme into a bowl. Pour over the hot water. Leave to soak for 30 minutes.

2 Pull the head from the body of each squid and remove the quill. Cut the tentacles from the head and rinse these under cold water. Pull off the outer skin, then cut the body into 5mm/ 1/4in rings. Cut the monkfish into 2.5cm/1in cubes.

3 Bring a large pan of lightly salted water to the boil. Put the garlic, onions and fennel into a separate pan and pour over the wine. Cover and simmer for 5 minutes until tender.

4 Add the monkfish to the onion mixture, then pour in the sun-dried tomato mixture. Cover and cook for 3 minutes, then add the prawns in their shells and squid. Cover and cook over a low heat for 1–2 minutes. Do not overcook or the squid will toughen. Season to taste with salt and pepper.

5 Meanwhile, add the pasta to the pan of boiling water and cook until al dente.

6 Drain the pasta, divide it among four warmed dishes and top with the fish and shellfish sauce. Sprinkle with the chopped parsley and serve at once.

Mixed Summer Pasta

A pretty sauce with plenty of flavour makes this a perfect dish for supper on a warm summer evening.

Serves 4
115g/4oz French beans, cut into
    2.5cm/1in pieces
350g/12oz dried fusilli lunghi
15ml/1 tbsp olive oil
1/2 fennel bulb, sliced
1 bunch spring onions,
    sliced diagonally
115g/4oz yellow cherry tomatoes
115g/4oz red cherry tomatoes
30ml/2 tbsp chopped fresh dill
225g/8oz cooked peeled prawns
15ml/1 tbsp lemon juice
15ml/1 tbsp wholegrain mustard
60ml/4 tbsp very low-fat
    fromage frais
salt and freshly ground
    black pepper
fresh dill sprigs, to garnish

1 Bring a large pan of lightly salted water to the boil and cook the beans for 5 minutes, until tender. Lift out with a slotted spoon, refresh under cold water and drain again. Set aside.

2 Bring the water back to the boil, add the pasta and cook until it is al dente.

3 Meanwhile, heat the oil in a large non-stick frying pan. Add the fennel and spring onions, and fry, stirring occasionally, for about 5 minutes.

4 Stir in the cherry tomatoes and fry for 5 minutes more, stirring occasionally.

5 Add the dill and prawns to the pan, cook for 1 minute, then stir in the lemon juice, mustard, fromage frais and beans. Season to taste and simmer for 1 minute.

6 Drain the pasta and add it to the prawn and vegetable sauce. Toss well. Serve immediately, garnished with the fresh dill.

Seafood Conchiglione with Spinach

Conchiglione are very large pasta shells, measuring about 4cm/1½in; don't try stuffing smaller shells – they're much too fiddly!

Serves 4

32 conchiglione
25g/1oz/2 tbsp low-fat spread,
    plus extra for greasing
8 spring onions, finely sliced
6 tomatoes, peeled and chopped

225g/8oz/1 cup low-fat
    soft cheese
90ml/6 tbsp skimmed milk
pinch of freshly grated nutmeg
225g/8oz cooked peeled prawns
175g/6oz can white crab meat,
    drained and flaked
115g/4oz frozen chopped
    spinach, thawed and drained
salt and freshly ground
    black pepper

1 Preheat the oven to 150°C/300°F/Gas 2. Bring a large pan of lightly salted water to the boil and cook the conchiglione for 10 minutes. Drain, rinse with boiling water, then drain again.

2 Melt the butter in a small saucepan. Add the spring onions and cook over a low heat, stirring occasionally, for 3–4 minutes, or until softened. Stir in the tomatoes and cook for a further 4–5 minutes.

3 Put the soft cheese and milk in a saucepan and heat gently, stirring until blended. Season to taste with salt, pepper and a pinch of nutmeg. Spoon 30ml/2 tbsp of the cheese sauce into a bowl and set the remainder aside.

4 Add the spring onion and tomato mixture to the sauce in the bowl, together with the prawns and flaked crab meat. Mix thoroughly.

5 Spoon the seafood filling into the pasta shells and place in a single layer in a lightly greased shallow ovenproof dish. Cover with foil and bake for 10 minutes.

6 Stir the spinach into the remaining cheese sauce. Bring to the boil, then simmer gently for 1 minute, stirring all the time. Drizzle over the filled conchiglione and serve hot.

Baked Seafood Pasta

So simple to make it's bound to become a family favourite, this is a wonderful way of serving pasta.

Serves 6

65g/2½ oz/5 tbsp low-fat spread,
    plus extra for greasing
225g/8oz dried fettuccine
25g/1oz/¼ cup plain flour
475ml/16fl oz/2 cups skimmed milk
2.5ml/½ tsp dried mustard

5ml/1 tsp lemon juice
15ml/1 tbsp tomato purée
½ onion, finely chopped
2 celery sticks, diced
115g/4oz/1¼ cups small
    mushrooms, sliced
225g/8oz cooked peeled shrimp
225g/8oz crab meat
15ml/1 tbsp chopped fresh dill
salt and freshly ground
    black pepper
fresh dill sprigs, to garnish

1 Preheat the oven to 180°C/350°F/Gas 4. Generously grease a large ovenproof dish with low-fat spread.

2 Bring a large pan of lightly salted water to the boil and cook the pasta until it is *al dente*.

3 Meanwhile, melt 40g/1½oz/3 tbsp of the low-fat spread in a saucepan. Stir in the flour and cook for 1 minute, stirring constantly, then gradually add the milk, stirring until the sauce boils and thickens.

4 Add the mustard, lemon juice and tomato purée to the sauce, and mix well. Season to taste with salt and pepper.

5 Melt the remaining low-fat spread in a frying pan. Add the onion, celery and mushrooms. Cook over a medium heat, stirring occasionally, for about 5 minutes, until softened.

6 Drain the pasta and tip it into a large mixing bowl. Add the sauce, vegetable mixture, shrimp, crab meat and chopped dill. Stir thoroughly.

7 Pour the mixture evenly into the prepared dish. Bake for 30–40 minutes, until the top is lightly browned. Garnish with the dill sprigs and serve immediately.

Pasta with Scallops in Warm Green Tartare Sauce

When you are trying not to eat too much fat, sauces can be the thing you miss most. Here is a deliciously creamy dish that won't compromise your conscience.

Serves 4
12 large scallops
350g/12oz dried black tagliatelle
60ml/4 tbsp white wine
150ml/ 1/4 pint/ 2/3 cup fish stock
lime wedges and parsley sprigs,
   to garnish

For the tartare sauce
120ml/4fl oz/ 1/2 cup low-fat
   crème fraîche
10ml/2 tsp wholegrain mustard
2 garlic cloves, crushed
30–45ml/2–3 tbsp freshly
   squeezed lime juice
60ml/4 tbsp chopped
   fresh parsley
30ml/2 tbsp snipped chives
salt and freshly ground
   black pepper

1 Slice the scallops in half, horizontally. Keep any corals whole. Set aside.

2 To make the tartare sauce, mix the crème fraîche, mustard, garlic, lime juice and herbs in a bowl. Season with salt and pepper to taste.

3 Bring a large pan of lightly salted water to the boil and cook the pasta until it is *al dente*.

4 Meanwhile, put the white wine and fish stock into a pan. Heat to simmering point. Add the scallops and cook very gently for 3–4 minutes (no longer or they will become tough).

5 Lift out the scallops with a slotted spoon. Boil the wine and stock to reduce by half, then add the tartare sauce to the pan. Heat gently, replace the scallops and cook for 1 minute.

6 Drain the pasta and divide it among four warmed bowls. Spoon the scallops and sauce over, garnish with lime wedges and parsley, and serve.

Devilled Crab Conchiglione

Large pasta shells are perfect for stuffing, and this is a really tasty filling.

Serves 4
350g/12oz/3 cups
   dried conchiglione
200g/7oz/scant 1 cup low-fat
   cream cheese
150ml/ 1/4 pint/ 2/3 cup
   skimmed milk
2.5ml/1/2 tsp ground paprika
5ml/1 tsp Dijon mustard
15ml/1 tbsp dried breadcrumbs
10ml/2 tsp freshly grated
   Parmesan cheese

For the filling
1 shallot, finely chopped
1 celery stick, finely chopped
1/2 small red pepper, seeded and
   finely chopped
45ml/3 tbsp white wine
45ml/3 tbsp low-fat crème fraîche
2 x 175g/6oz cans crab meat in
   brine, drained
45ml/3 tbsp fresh
   white breadcrumbs
30ml/2 tbsp freshly grated
   Parmesan cheese
15ml/1 tbsp Dijon mustard
2.5ml/ 1/2 tsp red chilli paste
salt and freshly ground
   black pepper

1 To make the filling, put the shallot, celery, red pepper and wine into a small pan, cover and cook gently for 3–4 minutes, until the vegetables are tender and little of the wine remains. Remove the pan from the heat and stir in the crème fraîche, crab meat, fresh breadcrumbs, Parmesan, mustard and chilli paste. Season, if necessary.

2 Bring a large pan of lightly salted water to the boil and cook the conchiglione, in batches if necessary, until *al dente*. Drain well, then arrange upside-down on a clean dish towel to dry.

3 Put the cream cheese, milk, paprika and mustard into a small pan. Heat gently and whisk until smooth. Season to taste. Pour the sauce into a large ovenproof dish.

4 Preheat the oven to 220°C/425°F/Gas 7. Fill the conchiglione with the crab mixture, and arrange them on top of the sauce. Mix the dried breadcrumbs and Parmesan, and sprinkle on top. Cover the dish with foil and bake for 15 minutes. Uncover and return to the oven for 5 minutes more. Serve at once.

Spaghetti with White Clam Sauce

This is a low-fat version of one of Italy's most famous pasta dishes.

Serves 4
1kg/2¼lb fresh clams
120ml/4fl oz/½ cup dry
  white wine
350g/12oz dried spaghetti
30ml/2 tbsp olive oil
2 whole garlic cloves, peeled
45ml/3 tbsp chopped fresh
  flat leaf parsley
salt and freshly ground
  black pepper

1 Scrub the clams under cold running water, discarding any that are open or that do not close when sharply tapped against the work surface.

2 Put the clams in a large pan, add the wine, then cover the pan tightly and place it over a high heat. Cook, shaking the pan frequently, for about 5 minutes, until the clams are opened.

3 Using a slotted spoon, transfer the clams to a bowl, discarding any that have failed to open. Strain the liquid and set it aside. Put 12 clams in their shells to one side for the garnish, then remove the rest from their shells.

4 Bring a large pan of lightly salted water to the boil and cook the pasta until it is *al dente*.

5 Meanwhile, heat the oil in a deep pan. Fry the whole garlic cloves over a medium heat until golden, crushing them with the back of a spoon. Remove the garlic with a slotted spoon and discard.

6 Add the shelled clams to the garlic-flavoured oil and moisten them with some of the strained liquid from the clams. Season with plenty of pepper. Cook for 1–2 minutes, gradually adding more liquid as the sauce reduces. Stir in the parsley and cook for a further 1–2 minutes.

7 Drain the pasta, add it to the pan and toss well. Serve in individual dishes, garnished with the reserved clams.

Black Pasta with Raw Vegetables

Black pasta derives its colour from the addition of squid ink and looks very dramatic with the colourful vegetables. The avocado will push up the fat content, so leave it out if you prefer.

Serves 4
3 garlic cloves, crushed
15ml/1 tbsp white
  tarragon vinegar
5ml/1 tsp Dijon mustard
30ml/2 tbsp extra virgin olive oil
5ml/1 tsp finely chopped
  fresh thyme
1 yellow pepper, seeded
1 red pepper, seeded
225g/8oz mangetouts, topped
  and tailed
6 radishes
4 ripe plum tomatoes, peeled
  and seeded
½ avocado (optional)
275g/10oz dried black pasta
salt and freshly ground
  black pepper
12 fresh basil leaves, to garnish

1 Make a dressing by whisking the garlic, vinegar, mustard, olive oil and chopped thyme together in a large bowl. Season to taste with salt and black pepper.

2 Cut the red and yellow peppers into diamond shapes, halve the mangetouts and slice the radishes.

3 Dice the tomatoes. Peel, stone and slice the avocado, if using. Place all the vegetables in a bowl and add the dressing, stirring thoroughly to mix.

4 Bring a large pan of lightly salted water to the boil and cook the pasta until *al dente*.

5 Drain and tip the pasta into a large shallow serving dish. Cover with the dressed vegetables and serve immediately, garnished with basil leaves.

Variation
Instead of black pasta, you could use Japanese soba or buckwheat noodles, which have a nutty flavour and texture.

Trenette with Shellfish

Colourful and delicious, this is ideal for a dinner party.

Serves 4
30ml/2 tbsp olive oil
1 small onion, finely chopped
1 garlic clove, crushed
½ fresh red chilli, seeded and chopped
200g/7oz can chopped tomatoes
30ml/2 tbsp chopped fresh parsley

400g/14oz live clams, scrubbed
400g/14oz live mussels, scrubbed and bearded
60ml/4 tbsp dry white wine
400g/14oz/3½ cups dried trenette
a few fresh basil leaves
90g/3½oz cooked peeled prawns
salt and freshly ground black pepper
chopped fresh herbs, to garnish

1 Heat 30ml/2 tbsp of the oil in a saucepan and cook the onion, garlic and chilli for 1–2 minutes. Stir in the tomatoes, half the parsley and pepper to taste. Bring to the boil, lower the heat, cover and simmer for 15 minutes.

2 Discard any shellfish that are open or that do not close when sharply tapped against the work surface. Heat the remaining oil in a large saucepan. Add the clams and mussels, with the rest of the parsley and toss over a high heat for a few seconds.

3 Pour in the wine, then cover tightly. Cook for 5 minutes, shaking the pan frequently, until the clams and mussels have opened. Using a slotted spoon, transfer them to a bowl, discarding any shellfish that have failed to open.

4 Strain the cooking liquid and set aside. Reserve some clams and mussels, then shell the rest. Bring a large pan of lightly salted water to the boil and cook the pasta until it is *al dente*.

5 Meanwhile, add 120ml/4fl oz/ ½ cup of the reserved seafood liquid to the tomato sauce. Bring to the boil, lower the heat, tear in the basil leaves and stir in the prawns and shellfish.

6 Drain the pasta and tip it into a warmed bowl. Add the seafood sauce and toss well. Serve in warmed bowls. Sprinkle each portion with herbs and garnish with the reserved shellfish.

Tagliolini with Mussels & Clams

This makes a stunning starter for a dinner party.

Serves 4
450g/1lb fresh clams, scrubbed
450g/1lb fresh mussels, scrubbed and bearded
30ml/2 tbsp olive oil
1 small onion, finely chopped
2 garlic cloves, finely chopped
1 large handful fresh flat leaf parsley, plus extra chopped parsley to garnish

175ml/6fl oz/ ¾ cup dry white wine
250ml/8fl oz/1 cup fish stock
1 small fresh red chilli, seeded and chopped
350g/12oz dried squid ink tagliolini
salt and freshly ground black pepper

1 Check the clams and mussels, and discard any that are open, or which fail to close when tapped on the work surface.

2 Heat half the oil in a saucepan and cook the onion until soft. Add the garlic, half the parsley and seasoning. Add the clams, mussels and wine, cover and bring to the boil. Cook for 5 minutes, shaking the pan frequently, until the shellfish have opened.

3 Drain the shellfish in a fine sieve set over a bowl. Discard the aromatics, with any shellfish that have failed to open. Return the strained liquid to the clean pan and add the stock. Chop the remaining parsley finely; add it to the pan with the chilli. Bring to the boil, then simmer, until slightly reduced. Turn off the heat.

4 Remove and discard the top shells from about half the clams and mussels. Put all the clams and mussels in the pan of liquid and seasonings, then cover the pan tightly and set aside.

5 Bring a large pan of lightly salted water to the boil and cook the pasta until *al dente*. Drain it, return it to the clean pan and toss with the remaining olive oil. Put the pan of shellfish over a high heat and toss to heat through. Divide the pasta among four warmed plates, spoon the shellfish mixture over, sprinkle with the extra parsley and serve.

Spaghetti Marinara

Shrimps, prawns and clams combine to make a superb seafood sauce which can be used with any type of pasta.

Serves 4

15ml/1 tbsp olive oil
1 medium onion, chopped
1 garlic clove, finely chopped
225g/8oz dried spaghetti
600ml/1 pint/2½ cups passata
15ml/1 tbsp tomato purée
5ml/1 tsp dried oregano
1 bay leaf

5ml/1 tsp sugar
115g/4oz/1 cup cooked
  peeled shrimps
115g/4oz/1 cup cooked
  peeled prawns
175g/6oz/1½ cups cooked clams
  or cockles, rinsed well if canned
  or bottled
15ml/1 tbsp lemon juice
45ml/3 tbsp chopped
  fresh parsley
15g/½oz/1 tbsp butter
salt and freshly ground
  black pepper

1 Heat the oil in a large saucepan and add the onion and garlic. Fry over a medium heat, stirring occasionally, for 6–7 minutes, until the onion has softened.

2 Bring a large saucepan of lightly salted water to the boil and cook the spaghetti until *al dente*.

3 Meanwhile, stir the passata, tomato purée, oregano, bay leaf and sugar into the onions, and season to taste with salt and pepper. Bring to the boil, then lower the heat and simmer for 2–3 minutes.

4 Add the shrimps, prawns, clams or cockles, lemon juice and 30ml/2 tbsp of the parsley to the passata mixture. Stir well, then cover and cook for 6–7 minutes.

5 Drain the spaghetti. Melt the butter in the clean pan. Return the drained pasta to the pan and toss with the butter. Season to taste with salt and pepper.

6 Divide the spaghetti among four warmed plates and top with the seafood sauce. Sprinkle with the remaining parsley and serve immediately.

Baked Seafood Spaghetti

Good things come in small packages, and in this case parchment parcels are opened at the table to reveal a tasty seafood and pasta filling.

Serves 4

450g/1lb live mussels, scrubbed
  and bearded
120ml/4fl oz/½ cup dry
  white wine

30ml/2 tbsp olive oil
2 garlic cloves, finely chopped
450g/1lb tomatoes, peeled and
  finely chopped
400g/14oz dried spaghetti or
  other long pasta
225g/8oz cooked peeled prawns
30ml/2 tbsp chopped
  fresh parsley
salt and freshly ground
  black pepper

1 Check the mussels, discarding any which are not tightly closed, or which fail to close when tapped on the work surface. Put them in a large pan with the wine. Cover the pan and place it over a moderate heat. As soon as the mussels open, lift them out with a slotted spoon. Discard any that remain closed.

2 Pour the cooking liquid through a strainer lined with kitchen paper, and reserve. Preheat the oven to 150°C/300°F/Gas 2.

3 Heat the oil in a medium saucepan and cook the garlic for 1–2 minutes. Add the tomatoes and cook until they soften. Stir in 175ml/6fl oz/¾ cup of the cooking liquid from the mussels.

4 Bring a large pan of lightly salted water to the boil. Add the spaghetti and cook until it is *al dente*.

5 When the pasta is almost cooked, add the prawns and parsley to the tomato sauce. Season and remove from the heat. Drain the pasta and mix it with the sauce and mussels.

6 Cut out four 45 x 30cm/18 x 12in pieces of non-stick baking paper. Divide the pasta and seafood mixture among them and twist the paper ends together to make a sealed packet. Arrange in a roasting tin and bake for 8–10 minutes. Place one unopened packet on each plate and serve.

Spaghetti with Clams

Clams, especially the hard-shell varieties and ocean quahogs, are particularly popular on the Atlantic seaboard of America, which is where this version of the well-known dish originated.

Serves 4

24 live clams, in their
  shells, scrubbed
250ml/8fl oz/1 cup water
120ml/4fl oz/ $\frac{1}{2}$ cup dry
  white wine
450g/1lb dried spaghetti
15ml/1 tbsp olive oil
2 garlic cloves, finely chopped
45ml/3 tbsp finely chopped
  fresh parsley
salt and freshly ground
  black pepper

1 Rinse the clams well in cold water and drain. Discard any that are open and do not shut when sharply tapped on a work surface. Place the clams in a large pan with the measured water and wine. Bring to the boil, cover and steam, shaking the pan frequently, for 6–8 minutes, or until the shells open.

2 Discard any clams that have not opened. Remove the rest from their shells. Cut off and discard the siphon from any large clams and roughly chop the flesh.

3 Pour the cooking liquid through a strainer lined with kitchen paper. Place in a small saucepan and boil rapidly until it has reduced by about half. Set aside.

4 Bring a large pan of lightly salted water to the boil. Add the spaghetti and cook until it is al dente.

5 Meanwhile, heat the olive oil in a large frying pan. Add the garlic and cook for 2–3 minutes, but do not let it brown. Add the reduced clam liquid and the parsley. Leave it to cook over low heat until the spaghetti is ready.

6 Drain the spaghetti. Add it to the frying pan, raise the heat to medium, and add the clams. Cook for 3–4 minutes, tossing the pasta with the sauce. Season to taste with salt and pepper, and serve immediately.

Linguine with Clam & Tomato Sauce

Simple and supremely satisfying, this classic Italian dish is low in fat, so will suit those who are watching their diet.

Serves 4

900g/2lb live clams in their
  shells, scrubbed
250ml/8fl oz/1 cup water
350g/12oz dried linguine
15ml/1 tbsp olive oil
1 garlic clove, crushed
400g/14oz tomatoes, fresh or
  canned, very finely chopped
60ml/4 tbsp chopped
  fresh parsley
salt and freshly ground
  black pepper

1 Rinse the clams well in cold water and drain. Discard any that are open and do not shut when sharply tapped on a work surface. Place them in a large saucepan with the measured water. Bring to the boil, cover and steam, for 6–8 minutes, until the shells open. Lift out the clams with a slotted spoon, discarding any that remain shut.

2 Remove the clams from their shells, adding any juices to the liquid in the pan. Cut off and discard the siphon from any large clams and chop the flesh into two or three pieces. Strain the cooking juices through a sieve lined with kitchen paper.

3 Bring a large pan of lightly salted water to the boil and cook the pasta until it is al dente. Meanwhile, heat the olive oil in a separate pan. Add the garlic and cook over a medium heat until the garlic is golden, then discard it.

4 Add the chopped tomatoes to the oil, and pour in the clam cooking liquid. Mix well and cook until the sauce begins to dry out and thicken slightly.

5 Stir the parsley and clams into the tomato sauce and increase the heat. Season to taste with pepper. Drain the pasta and tip it into a warmed serving bowl. Pour on the hot sauce and mix well before serving.

Soba Noodles with Nori

Tender noodles, crisp toasted seaweed and a savoury dipping sauce make for a simple, but delicious light meal.

Serves 4
350g/12oz dried soba noodles
1 sheet nori seaweed

For the dipping sauce
300ml/ ½ pint/1 ¼ cups
  bonito stock
120ml/4fl oz/ ½ cup dark
  soy sauce
60ml/4 tbsp mirin
5ml/1 tsp sugar
10g/ ¼ oz loose bonito flakes

For the flavourings
4 spring onions, finely chopped
30ml/2 tbsp grated
  mooli (daikon)
wasabi paste

1 Make the dipping sauce. Combine the stock, soy sauce, mirin and sugar in a saucepan. Bring rapidly to the boil, add the bonito flakes, then remove from the heat. When cool, strain the sauce into a bowl and cover.

2 Bring a pan of lightly salted water to the boil and cook the soba noodles for 6–7 minutes or until just tender, following the manufacturer's directions on the packet.

3 Drain the noodles and then rinse them under cold running water, agitating them gently to remove the excess starch. Drain well again.

4 Toast the nori over a high gas flame or under a preheated grill, then crumble into thin strips. Divide the noodles among four serving dishes and top with the nori. Serve each portion with an individual bowl of dipping sauce and offer the flavourings separately.

> **Cook's Tip**
> *The dipping sauce can be made up to a week before it is needed. Cover it and keep it in the fridge.*

Egg Noodles with Tuna & Tomato Sauce

Raid the store cupboard, add a few fresh ingredients and you can produce a scrumptious main meal in a matter of moments.

Serves 4
15ml/1 tbsp olive oil
2 garlic cloves, finely chopped
2 dried red chillies, seeded
  and chopped
1 large red onion, thinly sliced
175g/6oz can tuna in
  brine, drained
6–8 stoned black olives
400g/14oz can chopped
  tomatoes
30ml/2 tbsp chopped
  fresh parsley
350g/12oz medium-thick dried
  egg noodles
salt and freshly ground
  black pepper

1 Heat the oil in a large frying pan. Add the garlic and dried chillies, and fry for a few seconds, then add the sliced onion. Cook over a medium heat, stirring occasionally, for about 5 minutes, until the onion softens.

2 Add the tuna and olives to the pan, and stir until well mixed. Stir in the tomatoes, with any juices. Bring to the boil, season well, stir in the parsley, then lower the heat and simmer gently.

3 Meanwhile, bring a large pan of lightly salted water to the boil. Add the noodles and cook them until just tender, following the directions on the packet.

4 Drain the noodles well and return them to the clean pan. Add the sauce, toss to mix and serve immediately.

> **Cook's Tip**
> *Depending on the contents of your store cupboard, you could substitute other canned fish for the tuna. Try mackerel, sardines or salmon, for example. You could also add bottled clams or canned anchovies.*

Seafood & Vermicelli Stir-fry

Seafood is the perfect choice for stir-fries, as it requires the fastest of cooking and combines superbly with noodles.

Serves 4

450g/1lb rice vermicelli, soaked in
   warm water until soft
15ml/1 tbsp vegetable oil
50g/2oz/ ½ cup drained sun-
   dried tomatoes, reconstituted in
   water then drained and sliced
3 spring onions, sliced on
   the diagonal
2 large carrots, cut into batons
1 courgette, cut into batons
225g/8oz raw prawns, peeled
   and deveined
225g/8oz shelled scallops
2.5cm/1in piece of fresh root
   ginger, finely grated
45ml/3 tbsp lemon juice
45ml/3 tbsp chopped fresh basil
salt and freshly ground
   black pepper

1 Bring a large pan of lightly salted water to the boil. Add the rice vermicelli and cook until tender, following the instructions on the packet. Drain, rinse with boiling water, and drain again thoroughly. Keep warm.

2 Heat a wok, add the oil, then stir-fry the sun-dried tomatoes, spring onions and carrots over a high heat for 5 minutes.

3 Add the courgette, prawns, scallops and ginger. Stir-fry for 3 minutes.

4 Pour in the lemon juice. Add the basil, with salt and pepper to taste, and stir well. Stir-fry for 2 minutes more. Divide the rice vermicelli among individual plates and spoon the stir-fried mixture on top. Serve immediately.

> **Cook's Tip**
> The easiest way to prepare the carrots and courgette is to slice them lengthways, then cut them across in thin sticks. Don't make them matchstick-thin or they will overcook.

Buckwheat Noodles with Smoked Trout

The light, crisp texture of the pak choi balances the tender shiitake mushrooms and noodles and perfectly complements the delicate flesh of smoked trout.

Serves 4

350g/12oz buckwheat or
   soba noodles
15ml/1 tbsp vegetable oil
115g/4oz fresh shiitake
   mushrooms, quartered
2 garlic cloves, finely chopped
15ml/1 tbsp grated fresh
   root ginger
225g/8oz pak choi, trimmed and
   separated into leaves
1 spring onion, finely sliced on
   the diagonal
5ml/1 tsp dark sesame oil
30ml/2 tbsp mirin or dry sherry
30ml/2 tbsp soy sauce
2 smoked trout, skinned
   and boned
salt
30ml/2 tbsp coriander leaves and
   10ml/2 tsp toasted sesame
   seeds, to garnish

1 Bring a large pan of lightly salted water to the boil and cook the buckwheat or soba noodles until just tender, following the instructions on the packet.

2 Meanwhile, heat a wok until hot, add the oil and swirl it around. Add the shiitake mushrooms and stir-fry over a medium heat for 3 minutes.

3 Add the garlic, ginger and pak choi and toss over the heat for a further 2 minutes.

4 Drain the noodles very well and add them to the mushroom mixture, together with the spring onion, sesame oil, mirin or sherry and soy sauce. Stir briefly until heated through.

5 Break the smoked trout into bite-size pieces. Arrange the noodle mixture on individual serving plates. Place the smoked trout on top, garnish with coriander leaves and sesame seeds, and serve immediately.

Noodles with Prawns in Lemon Sauce

In this Chinese dish, it is the noodles that are the prime ingredient, with seafood playing a minor, but still important, role in terms of flavour and colour.

Serves 4
2 packets dried egg noodles
15ml/1 tbsp sunflower oil
2 celery sticks, cut
   into matchsticks
2 garlic cloves, crushed
4 spring onions, sliced
2 carrots, cut into matchsticks
7.5cm/3in piece of cucumber, cut
   into matchsticks
115g/4oz raw prawns, in
   their shells
pared rind and juice of 1 lemon
5ml/1 tsp cornflour
60–75ml/4–5 tbsp fish stock
115g/4oz/1 cup cooked
   peeled prawns
salt and freshly ground
   black pepper
fresh dill sprigs, to garnish

1 Bring a large pan of lightly salted water to the boil and cook the noodles until tender.

2 Meanwhile, heat the oil in a pan and stir-fry the celery, garlic, spring onions and carrots for 2–3 minutes. Add the cucumber and shell-on prawns, and cook for 2–3 minutes. Blanch the pared lemon rind in boiling water for 1 minute.

3 Mix the lemon juice with the cornflour and stock, and add to the pan. Bring gently to the boil, stirring, and cook for 1 minute.

4 Drain the lemon rind and add it to the pan, with the peeled prawns. Season to taste. Drain the noodles and serve with the prawn sauce. Garnish each portion with dill.

> **Cook's Tip**
> *Dried egg noodles need very little cooking. In some cases you just immerse them in boiling water for a few minutes. Always check the instructions on the packet.*

Chilli Squid & Noodles

In China, this popular noodle dish is traditionally cooked in a clay pot.

Serves 4
675g/1½ lb prepared squid
15ml/1 tbsp vegetable oil
3 slices of fresh root ginger,
   finely shredded
2 garlic cloves, finely chopped
1 red onion, thinly sliced
1 carrot, thinly sliced
1 celery stick, sliced
50g/2oz/⅓ cup sugar snap peas,
   topped and tailed
5ml/1 tsp sugar
15ml/1 tbsp chilli bean paste
2.5ml/½ tsp chilli powder
75g/3oz cellophane noodles,
   soaked in warm water until soft
120ml/4fl oz/½ cup light
   chicken stock
15ml/1 tbsp soy sauce
15ml/1 tbsp oyster sauce
5ml/1 tsp sesame oil
salt
fresh coriander leaves, to garnish

1 Cut the body of the squid into rings or split it open lengthways, score criss-cross patterns on the inside of the body and cut it into 5 x 4cm/2 x 1½in pieces.

2 Heat the oil in a flameproof casserole. Add the ginger, garlic and onion, and fry, stirring occasionally, for 1–2 minutes.

3 Add the squid, carrot, celery and sugar snap peas. Fry until the squid curls up. Season with salt to taste and stir in the sugar, chilli bean paste and chilli powder. Transfer the mixture to a bowl and set aside.

4 Drain the soaked noodles and add them to the casserole. Stir in the stock and sauces. Cover and cook for 10 minutes, or until the noodles are tender.

5 Return the squid and vegetables to the casserole. Cover and cook for about 5–6 minutes more, until all the flavours are combined. Serve in warmed bowls.

6 Drizzle each portion with sesame oil and sprinkle with the coriander leaves.

Sweet & Sour Prawns with Noodles

Chinese dried noodles need very little cooking. Use one skein per person.

Serves 4–6

15g/ ½oz/ ¼ cup Chinese dried mushrooms
300ml/ ½ pint/1 ¼ cups hot water
1 bunch of spring onions, cut into thick diagonal slices
2.5cm/1in piece of fresh root ginger, grated
1 red pepper, seeded and diced
225g/8oz can water chestnuts, sliced
45ml/3 tbsp light soy sauce
30ml/2 tbsp sherry
350g/12oz large cooked peeled prawns
225g/8oz dried egg noodles

1 Put the Chinese dried mushrooms into a bowl. Pour over the measured hot water and set aside to soak for 15 minutes.

2 Strain the soaking liquid through a fine sieve into a pan. Chop the mushrooms and add them to the pan, with the spring onions, ginger and diced red pepper. Bring to the boil, lower the heat, cover and cook for about 5 minutes, until the vegetables are tender.

3 Add the water chestnuts, soy sauce, sherry and prawns to the vegetable mixture. Cover and cook gently for 2 minutes.

4 Meanwhile, bring a large pan of lightly salted water to the boil. Add the noodles and cook them until just tender, checking the packet for information on timing. Drain thoroughly and tip into a warmed serving dish. Spoon the sweet and sour prawns on top and toss to mix. Serve at once.

Cook's Tip

The Chinese vegetable water chestnuts (ma taai) are small corms with crisp white flesh and dark brown skins. They are sometimes available fresh and should be carefully peeled before use. Confusingly, there is a Chinese nut also known as the water chestnut (ling gok), but this is quite different.

Spicy Singapore Noodles

A delicious supper dish with a stunning mix of flavours and textures, as well as a hint of spiciness.

Serves 4

225g/8oz dried egg noodles
15ml/1 tbsp groundnut oil
1 onion, chopped
2.5cm/1in piece of fresh root ginger, finely chopped
1 garlic clove, finely chopped
15ml/1 tbsp Madras curry powder
115g/4oz cooked chicken or pork, finely shredded
115g/4oz cooked peeled prawns
115g/4oz Chinese cabbage leaves, shredded
115g/4oz/2 cups beansprouts
60ml/4 tbsp defatted chicken stock
15–30ml/1–2 tbsp dark soy sauce
salt
1–2 fresh red chillies, seeded and finely shredded and 4 spring onions, finely shredded, to garnish

1 Bring a large pan of lightly salted water to the boil and cook the noodles until they are just tender, checking the packet for information on timing.

2 Rinse the noodles thoroughly under cold water and drain well. Add 5ml/1 tsp of the oil, toss lightly and set aside.

3 Preheat a wok and swirl in the remaining oil. When it is hot, add the onion, ginger and garlic, and stir-fry over a medium heat for about 2 minutes.

4 Stir in the curry powder and 2.5ml/½ tsp salt, stir-fry for 30 seconds, then add the drained noodles, chicken or pork and prawns. Stir-fry for 3–4 minutes.

5 Add the shredded Chinese cabbage and beansprouts, and stir-fry for 1–2 minutes more. Sprinkle in the stock and soy sauce to taste, and toss well until evenly mixed and heated through. Divide among warmed individual serving bowls or plates, garnish with the shredded red chillies and spring onions, and serve immediately.

POULTRY & MEAT

Orecchiette with Bacon & Chicken Livers

Sherry balances the saltiness of the bacon in this superbly rich sauce.

Serves 4
350g/12oz/3 cups
   dried orecchiette
225g/8oz frozen chicken livers,
   thawed and drained
15ml/1 tbsp olive oil
175g/6oz rindless lean smoked
   back bacon, roughly chopped
2 garlic cloves, crushed

400g/14oz can
   chopped tomatoes
150ml/¼ pint/⅔ cup
   chicken stock
15ml/1 tbsp tomato purée
15ml/1 tbsp dry sherry
30ml/2 tbsp chopped fresh
   mixed herbs
salt and freshly ground
   black pepper
freshly grated Parmesan
   cheese, to serve (optional)

1 Bring a large pan of lightly salted water to the boil and cook the pasta until it is al dente.

2 Meanwhile, trim the chicken livers and cut them into bite-size pieces. Heat the olive oil in a sauté pan, add the bacon and fry for 3–4 minutes.

3 Add the garlic and chicken livers to the pan and fry for a further 2–3 minutes. Stir in the tomatoes, chicken stock, tomato purée, sherry and herbs, and season with salt and pepper.

4 Bring to the boil, then lower the heat and simmer gently, uncovered, for about 5 minutes, until the sauce has thickened.

5 Drain the pasta, return it to the clean pan and toss it with the sauce. Serve hot, sprinkled with Parmesan cheese, if using.

Variation
You could substitute smoked or unsmoked pancetta for the back bacon, if you prefer.

Tagliatelle with Chicken & Vermouth

Vermouth gives this chicken sauce a delicious flavour, with the fromage frais taking the edge off the acidity.

Serves 4
15ml/1 tbsp olive oil
1 red onion, cut into wedges
350g/12oz dried tagliatelle
1 garlic clove, chopped
350g/12oz skinless, boneless
   chicken breasts, diced

300ml/½ pint/1¼ cups
   dry vermouth
45ml/3 tbsp chopped fresh
   mixed herbs
150ml/¼ pint/⅔ cup very-low-
   fat fromage frais
salt and freshly ground
   black pepper
shredded fresh mint, to garnish

1 Heat the oil in a large heavy-based frying pan. Add the onion and fry for about 10 minutes, until it starts to soften and the layers separate.

2 Bring a large pan of lightly salted water to the boil and cook the pasta until it is al dente.

3 Meanwhile, add the garlic and chicken to the onion and fry, stirring occasionally, for 10 minutes, until the chicken has browned all over and is cooked through.

4 Pour in the vermouth, bring to the boil and boil rapidly until reduced by about half. Stir in the herbs and fromage frais, and season with salt and pepper to taste. Heat through gently, but do not let the sauce boil.

5 Drain the pasta, return it to the clean pan and toss it with the sauce to coat. Serve in warmed bowls, garnished with the shredded mint.

Variation
If you don't want to use vermouth, use dry white wine instead. Orvieto or Frascati would be ideal.

Round Ravioli with Bolognese Sauce

Tender ravioli and a richly
flavoured, low-fat sauce –
what more could anyone
wish for?

Serves 6

225g/8oz/1 cup low-fat
   cottage cheese
30ml/2 tbsp grated Parmesan
   cheese, plus extra for serving
1 egg white, beaten, plus extra
   for brushing
1.5ml/ ¼ tsp freshly
   grated nutmeg
1 quantity of Basic Pasta Dough
flour, for dusting
salt and freshly ground
   black pepper

For the Bolognese Sauce

1 medium onion, finely chopped
1 garlic clove, crushed
150ml/ ¼ pint/ ⅔ cup defatted
   beef stock
350g/12oz minced turkey
120ml/4fl oz/ ½ cup red wine
30ml/2 tbsp tomato purée
400g/14oz can
   chopped tomatoes
2.5ml/ ½ tsp chopped
   fresh rosemary
1.5ml/ ¼ tsp ground allspice

1 To make the filling, mix the cottage cheese, grated Parmesan and egg white in a bowl, add the nutmeg, and season with salt and pepper to taste.

2 Roll the pasta into thin sheets. To make the ravioli, place small amounts of filling (about 5ml/1 tsp) in rows on half the pasta sheets at intervals of 5cm/2in.

3 Brush beaten egg white around each mound of filling. Top each sheet of filled pasta with a sheet of plain pasta and press between each pocket to remove any air and seal firmly.

4 Using a fluted ravioli or pastry cutter, stamp out rounds from the filled pasta and place these on a floured dish towel to dry while you make the sauce.

5 Put the onion and garlic in a pan. Add the stock and cook over a medium heat until most of it has been absorbed. Stir in the turkey and cook quickly to brown, breaking up any lumps with a fork.

6 Stir in the wine, tomato purée, chopped tomatoes, rosemary and allspice, and bring to the boil. Lower the heat and simmer, stirring occasionally, for 1 hour. Adjust the seasoning to taste.

7 Bring a large pan of lightly salted water to the boil and cook the ravioli, in batches if necessary, until *al dente*. Drain thoroughly. Serve topped with the Bolognese sauce. Hand grated Parmesan cheese separately.

> **Cook's Tip**
> *If you buy steak in a piece and mince it yourself, you will be sure that it is lean. Although supermarkets often label minced beef "extra lean" or "premium quality", these terms have no legal meaning. As a general rule, the lighter the colour of the mince, the more fat it contains.*

Spinach Tagliarini with Chicken & Asparagus

With its delicate colours
and fresh flavours, this
would be a good choice
for an *al fresco* supper in
early summer.

Serves 4–6

2 skinless, boneless
   chicken breasts
15ml/1 tbsp light soy sauce
30ml/2 tbsp sherry
30ml/2 tbsp cornflour
8 spring onions, trimmed and cut
   diagonally into 2.5cm/1in slices

1–2 garlic cloves, crushed
needle shreds of rind of ½ lemon
150ml/ ¼ pint/ ⅔ cup defatted
   chicken stock
5ml/1 tsp caster sugar
30ml/2 tbsp lemon juice
225g/8oz slender asparagus
   spears, trimmed and cut in
   7.5cm/3in lengths
450g/1lb fresh tagliarini
salt and freshly ground
   black pepper

1 Place the chicken breasts between two sheets of clear film and flatten each of them to a thickness of about 5mm/ ¼in with a rolling pin or the flat side of a meat mallet.

2 Cut the chicken across the grain into 2.5cm/1in strips. Put these into a bowl and add the soy sauce, sherry and cornflour, and season with plenty of salt and pepper. Toss well to coat each piece.

3 Put the chicken, spring onions, garlic and lemon rind in a large non-stick frying pan. Add the stock and bring to the boil, stirring constantly until thickened. Stir in the caster sugar, lemon juice and asparagus. Simmer over a low heat, stirring occasionally, for 4–5 minutes until tender.

4 Meanwhile, bring a large pan of lightly salted water to the boil and cook the pasta until *al dente*.

5 Drain the tagliarini thoroughly. Divide it among warmed serving plates, and spoon over the chicken and asparagus sauce. Serve immediately.

Penne with Spinach

If you love spinach you'll really enjoy this moist and appetizing pasta dish.

Serves 4
225g/8oz fresh spinach leaves
150g/5oz smoked turkey rashers
350g/12oz/3 cups dried penne, preferably mixed colours
1 garlic clove, crushed
1 small onion, finely chopped
½ small red pepper, seeded and finely chopped
1 small fresh red chilli, seeded and chopped
150ml/¼ pint/⅔ cup vegetable stock
45ml/3 tbsp low-fat crème fraîche
30ml/2 tbsp freshly grated Parmesan cheese, plus extra to garnish
crusty bread, to serve

1 Preheat the grill. Wash the spinach leaves and remove the hard central stalks. Shred the leaves finely and set them aside.

2 Cook the smoked turkey rashers under a preheated moderate grill for 3–4 minutes, until lightly browned. Let them cool a little, then chop them finely.

3 Bring a large pan of lightly salted water to the boil and cook the pasta until it is *al dente*.

4 Meanwhile, put the garlic, onion, red pepper and chilli into a large frying pan. Pour over the stock, cover and cook for about 5 minutes, or until the onion is tender. Add the prepared spinach and cook quickly for 2–3 minutes until it has wilted.

5 Drain the pasta and return it to the clean pan. Add the spinach mixture, the crème fraîche and the grated Parmesan. Toss gently but thoroughly, then pile on warmed plates, sprinkle with the chopped turkey and top with the extra Parmesan. Serve immediately with crusty bread.

> **Variation**
> *Substitute rocket for the spinach, omit the chilli and add a finely chopped, peeled and seeded tomato.*

Pasta Bonbons

For a special occasion, these pretty little pasta packages would be a fine choice.

Serves 4–6
1 quantity of Basic Pasta Dough
flour, for dusting
1 egg white, beaten
salt and freshly ground black pepper

For the filling
1 small onion, finely chopped
1 garlic clove, crushed
150ml/¼ pint/⅔ cup defatted chicken stock
225g/8oz minced turkey
2–3 fresh sage leaves, chopped
2 drained canned anchovy fillets

For the sauce
150ml/¼ pint/⅔ cup defatted chicken stock
200g/7oz/scant 1 cup low-fat cream cheese
15ml/1 tbsp lemon juice
5ml/1 tsp caster sugar
2 tomatoes, peeled, seeded and finely diced
½ red onion, finely chopped
6 small cornichons (pickled gherkins), sliced

1 Make the filling. Put the onion, garlic and stock into a pan. Bring to the boil, cover and simmer for 5 minutes, until the onion is tender. Uncover and boil for about 5 minutes, or until the stock has reduced to 30ml/2 tbsp.

2 Add the minced turkey and stir it over the heat until lightly coloured. Add the sage and anchovy fillets, and season to taste with salt and pepper. Cook uncovered for 5 minutes, until all the liquid has been absorbed. Leave to cool.

3 Divide the pasta dough in half. Roll one half into thin sheets and cut into 9 x 6cm/3½ x 2½in rectangles. Lay these on a lightly floured dish towel and repeat with the remaining dough.

4 Place a heaped teaspoon of the filling on the centre of each rectangle, brush the surrounding dough with beaten egg white and roll up the pasta to make bonbons or small crackers, pinching in the ends. Transfer to a floured dish towel and leave to rest for 1 hour before cooking.

5 To make the sauce, put the stock, cream cheese, lemon juice and sugar into a pan. Heat gently and whisk until smooth. Add the diced tomatoes, onion and cornichons, and leave over a low heat while you cook the bonbons.

6 Bring a large pan of lightly salted water to the boil and cook the bonbons, in batches, for 5 minutes. As each batch becomes tender, lift out the bonbons with a slotted spoon, drain well and drop into the sauce. When all the bonbons have been added, simmer them in the sauce for 2–3 minutes. Serve in warmed bowls, spooning a little sauce over each bonbon.

> **Cook's Tip**
> *Allow plenty of time for making these. The bonbons need to rest for at least an hour before being cooked.*

Low-fat Spaghetti alla Carbonara

Smoked turkey rashers make a good substitute for bacon in this new look at an old favourite.

Serves 4

150g/5oz smoked turkey rashers
1 medium onion, chopped
1–2 garlic cloves, crushed
150ml/ ¼ pint/ ⅔ cup vegetable
   stock or defatted chicken stock
450g/1lb chilli and garlic-
   flavoured spaghetti
150ml/ ¼ pint/ ⅔ cup dry
   white wine
200g/7oz/scant 1 cup low-fat
   cream cheese
30ml/2 tbsp chopped
   fresh parsley
salt and freshly ground
   black pepper
shavings of Parmesan cheese,
   to serve

1 Cut the turkey rashers into 1cm/ ½in strips. Dry-fry in a non-stick pan over a medium heat for 2–3 minutes.

2 Add the onion, garlic and stock to the pan. Bring to the boil, lower the heat, cover and simmer while you cook the pasta.

3 Bring a large pan of lightly salted water to the boil and cook the pasta until it is al dente.

4 Meanwhile, add the wine to the turkey mixture and bring to the boil. Boil rapidly until reduced by half.

5 Whisk the cream cheese into the turkey mixture, beating until smooth. Season to taste with salt and pepper.

6 Drain the pasta, return it to the clean pan, and add the sauce and the chopped parsley. Toss well. Serve immediately in warmed bowls, with shavings of Parmesan.

> **Cook's Tip**
> Add the cream cheese gradually, a spoonful at a time, when making the sauce.

Turkey & Pasta Bake

Low in fat, turkey is a good choice for healthy family meals. Here it is combined with smoked turkey rashers, vegetables and rigatoni and topped with cheese before being baked in the oven.

Serves 4

275g/10oz minced turkey
150g/5oz smoked turkey
   rashers, chopped
1–2 garlic cloves, crushed
1 onion, finely chopped
2 carrots, diced
30ml/2 tbsp tomato purée
300ml/ ½ pint/1 ¼ cups defatted
   chicken stock
225g/8oz/2 cups dried rigatoni
30ml/2 tbsp freshly grated
   Parmesan cheese
salt and freshly ground
   black pepper

1 Dry-fry the minced turkey in a non-stick pan over a medium heat, breaking up any large pieces with a wooden spoon, until well browned all over.

2 Add the chopped turkey rashers, garlic, onion, carrots, tomato purée and stock. Bring to the boil, cover and simmer for 1 hour until tender. Season, if necessary.

3 Preheat the oven to 180°C/350°F/Gas 4. Bring a large pan of lightly salted water to the boil and cook the pasta until al dente.

4 Drain thoroughly, return to the clean pan and mix with the turkey sauce.

5 Spoon the pasta mixture into a shallow ovenproof dish and sprinkle with the freshly grated Parmesan. Bake for 20–30 minutes. Let stand for 5 minutes before serving.

> **Cook's Tip**
> To remove the fat from home-made chicken stock, let it cool, then chill it overnight in the fridge. The fat will solidify on top and will easily be lifted off.

Spaghetti with Turkey Ragoût

Turkey mince is much lower in fat than most other meats and makes an excellent basis for a low-fat pasta meal.

Serves 4
450g/1lb minced turkey
1 medium onion, finely diced
1 medium carrot, diced
1 celery stick, diced
400g/14oz can chopped
   tomatoes
15ml/1 tbsp tomato purée
5ml/1 tsp dried oregano
2 bay leaves, plus extra
   to garnish
225g/8oz dried spaghetti
salt and freshly ground
   black pepper

1 In a non-stick pan, dry-fry the minced turkey with the diced onion over a medium heat, stirring frequently, until the mince is lightly coloured.

2 Stir in the carrot and celery, and cook, stirring constantly, for 5–8 minutes.

3 Add the tomatoes, tomato purée, dried oregano and bay leaves. Bring to the boil, lower the heat, cover and simmer for 40 minutes, until the sauce is thick and full of flavour. Season to taste with salt and pepper.

4 Meanwhile, bring a large pan of lightly salted water to the boil and cook the spaghetti until *al dente*.

5 Drain well, divide among warmed bowls, spoon the ragoût over and serve immediately garnished with bay leaves.

> **Cook's tip**
> *If you can't find minced turkey, use lean pork, lamb or beef mince and pour off all the fat from the pan before adding the vegetables.*

Piquant Chicken with Spaghetti

Morsels of tender chicken in a mouthwatering sauce make this a popular dish for all the family.

Serves 4
1 onion, finely chopped
1 carrot, diced
1 garlic clove, crushed
300ml/½ pint/1¼ cups
   vegetable stock
4 small skinless, boneless
   chicken breasts
1 bouquet garni
115g/4oz/1½ cups button
   mushrooms, thinly sliced
5ml/1 tsp balsamic vinegar
½ cucumber, peeled and cut
   into batons
350g/12oz dried spaghetti
2 firm ripe tomatoes, peeled,
   seeded and chopped
30ml/2 tbsp low-fat crème fraîche
15ml/1 tbsp chopped
   fresh parsley
15ml/1 tbsp snipped chives
salt and freshly ground
   black pepper

1 Put the onion, carrot, garlic and stock into a pan, and add the chicken breasts and bouquet garni. Bring to the boil, lower the heat, cover and simmer gently for 15–20 minutes, or until tender. Transfer the chicken to a plate and cover with foil.

2 Strain the cooking liquid into a clean pan, discarding the vegetables and flavourings. Add the sliced mushrooms and balsamic vinegar, and simmer for 2–3 minutes, until tender. Using a slotted spoon, lift out the mushrooms and set them aside. Boil the stock until it is reduced by half.

3 Meanwhile, bring a large pan of lightly salted water to the boil. Add the cucumber, cook for 20 seconds, then lift out and set aside. Add the pasta to the boiling water and cook it until it is *al dente*.

4 Cut the chicken breasts into bite-size pieces and stir them into the reduced stock, with the chopped tomatoes, crème fraîche, cucumber, parsley and chives. Season with salt and pepper to taste.

5 Drain the pasta, tip it into a warmed serving dish and spoon over the piquant chicken. Serve at once.

Rolled Stuffed Cannelloni

For tender, rustic-looking cannelloni, roll your own. Use lasagne sheets rather than rigid cannelloni tubes.

Serves 4

12 fresh or dried lasagne sheets
fresh basil leaves, to garnish

For the filling

2–3 garlic cloves, crushed
1 small onion, finely chopped
150ml/ ¼ pint/ ⅔ cup
   white wine
450g/1lb minced turkey
15ml/1 tbsp dried basil
15ml/1 tbsp dried thyme

40g/1½ oz/ ¾ cup fresh
   white breadcrumbs
salt and freshly ground
   black pepper

For the sauce

25g/1oz/2 tbsp low-fat margarine
25g/1oz/ ¼ cup plain flour
300ml/ ½ pint/1¼ cups
   skimmed milk
4 sun-dried tomatoes, soaked in
   warm water until soft, then
   drained and chopped
15ml/1 tbsp mixed chopped
   fresh herbs
30ml/2 tbsp freshly grated
   Parmesan cheese

1 First, make the filling. Put the garlic, onion and half the wine into a large pan. Cover and cook over a low heat for 5 minutes, then increase the heat and add the turkey. Cook it quickly, breaking up any lumps with a wooden spoon, until all the liquid has evaporated.

2 Lower the heat, and add the remaining wine and the herbs. Cover and cook for 20 minutes.

3 Draw the pan off the heat, stir in the breadcrumbs and season with salt and pepper to taste. Set aside to cool.

4 Bring a large pan of lightly salted water to the boil and cook the lasagne sheets, in batches if necessary, until *al dente*. Drain thoroughly, rinse in cold water and drain again. Pat dry on a clean dish towel.

5 Lay each lasagne sheet in turn on a board. Spoon turkey mixture along one short edge and roll it up to make a tube, encasing the filling. Cut the tubes in half.

6 Preheat the oven to 200°C/400°F/Gas 6. Make the sauce. Put the margarine, flour and skimmed milk into a pan, and whisk over a low heat until smooth. Add the tomatoes and mixed herbs, and season to taste with salt and pepper.

7 Spoon a thin layer of the sauce into a large, shallow ovenproof dish and arrange a layer of cannelloni on top, seam side down. Spoon a layer of sauce over the top, and cover with another layer of cannelloni and the remaining sauce. Sprinkle with grated Parmesan.

8 Bake for 10–15 minutes until lightly browned. Serve at once, garnished with fresh basil leaves.

Low-fat Lasagne

Serve this delicious lasagne with a garnish of mixed salad leaves.

Serves 6–8

1 large onion, chopped
2 garlic cloves, crushed
500g/1¼ lb minced turkey
450ml/ ¾ pint/1¾ cups passata
5ml/1 tsp mixed dried herbs
200g/7oz no-precook dried green
   lasagne sheets
200g/7oz/scant 1 cup low-fat
   cottage cheese
225g/8oz frozen leaf spinach,
   thawed and drained

For the sauce

25g/1oz/2 tbsp low-fat margarine
25g/1oz/ ¼ cup plain flour
300ml/ ½ pint/1¼ cups
   skimmed milk
25g/1oz/ ⅓ cup freshly grated
   Parmesan cheese
1.5ml/ ¼ tsp freshly
   grated nutmeg
salt and freshly ground
   black pepper
salad leaves and tomatoes,
   to serve

1 Put the onion, garlic and minced turkey into a non-stick saucepan. Cook over a medium heat, stirring with a wooden spoon to break up any lumps, for 5 minutes or until the turkey is lightly browned.

2 Add the passata and dried herbs, and season with salt and pepper to taste. Bring to the boil, then lower the heat. Cover and simmer for 30 minutes.

3 To make the sauce, put the margarine, flour and skimmed milk in a pan and whisk constantly over a low heat until the sauce boils and thickens. Stir in the Parmesan until melted. Stir in the nutmeg, and season with salt and pepper to taste.

4 Preheat the oven to 190°C/375°F/Gas 5. Layer the turkey mixture, lasagne sheets, cottage cheese and spinach in an ovenproof dish, starting and ending with a layer of turkey.

5 Spoon the cheese sauce evenly over the top and bake for 45–50 minutes, or until golden and bubbling. Leave to stand for 10–15 minutes before serving with salad leaves and tomatoes.

Penne with Chicken & Ham Sauce

A meal in itself, this colourful pasta dish is perfect for lunch or dinner.

Serves 4
350g/12oz/3 cups dried penne
15g/½oz/1 tbsp butter
1 onion, chopped
1 garlic clove, chopped
1 bay leaf
450ml/¾ pint/1¾ cups dry
  white wine
150ml/¼ pint/⅔ cup low-fat
  crème fraîche
225g/8oz cooked chicken,
  skinned, boned and diced
115g/4oz cooked lean
  ham, diced
50g/2oz/½ cup grated reduced-
  fat Gouda cheese
15ml/1 tbsp chopped fresh mint,
  plus extra to garnish
salt and freshly ground
  black pepper

1 Bring a pan of lightly salted water to the boil and cook the pasta until it is *al dente*.

2 Meanwhile, melt the butter in a large frying pan. Add the onion and fry over a medium heat, stirring occasionally, for 5 minutes, until softened. Add the garlic, bay leaf and wine and bring to the boil. Boil rapidly until reduced by half.

3 Remove and discard the bay leaf, then stir in the crème fraîche, chicken, ham and grated cheese. Lower the heat and simmer for 5 minutes, stirring occasionally, until heated through. Do not let the sauce boil. Stir in the chopped mint and season to taste with salt and pepper.

4 Drain the pasta and return it to the clean pan. Add the chicken and ham sauce, and toss well. Serve immediately in warmed bowls, garnished with the extra chopped mint.

Variations
• *Soured cream can be used instead of crème fraîche, or use 75g/3oz/6 tbsp cream cheese, thinned with a little milk.*
• *Cooked turkey can be used instead of the chicken and Parma ham instead of cooked ham.*

Fusilli with Turkey & Roasted Tomatoes

Roasting tomatoes gives them a depth of flavour that is delicious with the pasta and broccoli.

Serves 4–6
675g/1½lb ripe but firm plum
  tomatoes, quartered
30ml/2 tbsp olive oil
5ml/1 tsp dried oregano
350g/12oz broccoli florets
450g/1lb/4 cups dried fusilli
1 small onion, sliced
5ml/1 tsp dried thyme
450g/1lb skinless, boneless turkey
  breast, cubed
3 garlic cloves, crushed
15ml/1 tbsp lemon juice
salt and freshly ground
  black pepper

1 Preheat the oven to 200°C/400°F/Gas 6. Place the tomato quarters in a single layer in an ovenproof dish. Add 15ml/1 tbsp of the olive oil, the oregano and 2.5ml/1 tsp salt, and stir to mix. Roast, without stirring, for 30–40 minutes, until the tomatoes are just browned.

2 Meanwhile, bring a large pan of lightly salted water to the boil. Add the broccoli and cook for 5 minutes until just tender. Using a slotted spoon, transfer the broccoli to a colander, refresh it under cold water and leave it to drain. Reserve the pan of water.

3 Bring the reserved water back to the boil, add the pasta and cook it until it is *al dente*.

4 Meanwhile, heat the remaining oil in a large frying pan. Add the onion, thyme and turkey. Cook over a high heat, stirring often, for 5–7 minutes, until the meat is cooked.

5 Add the garlic and cook for 1 further minute, stirring frequently, then stir in the lemon juice and broccoli. Season with pepper and keep hot.

6 Drain the pasta, return it to the clean pan and toss it with the sauce. Serve at once in warmed bowls.

Pasta with Sausage, Corn & Red Peppers

This Italian-American recipe cleverly combines reduced fat with all the flavour of traditional ingredients in this quick and easy supper dish.

Serves 4
350g/12oz/3 cups dried fusilli
   or eliche
15ml/1 tbsp olive oil
1 onion, chopped
1 garlic clove, finely chopped
2 red peppers, seeded and sliced
250g/9oz/1½ cups frozen
   sweetcorn kernels, thawed
1 reduced-fat U-shaped smoked
   pork sausage
15ml/1 tbsp chopped fresh basil
salt and freshly ground
   black pepper
fresh basil sprigs, to garnish

1 Bring a large pan of lightly salted water to the boil and cook the pasta until it is *al dente*.

2 Meanwhile, heat the oil in a frying pan. Add the onion, garlic and red peppers, and cook over a medium heat, stirring frequently, for 5 minutes, until the onion is softened.

3 Stir in the sweetcorn kernels and heat through gently, stirring occasionally, for about 5 minutes. Season with salt and pepper to taste.

4 Heat the U-shaped sausage in a pan of simmering water, following the instructions on the packet. Do not allow the water to boil, as this will cause the skin to split. Alternatively, heat the sausage in the microwave, following the instructions on the packet.

5 Drain the sausage if necessary, remove the outer covering and slice the meat thinly. Stir the slices into the onion and pepper mixture.

6 Drain the pasta and return it to the clean pan. Add the sauce and chopped basil. Toss well. Serve in a warmed bowl, garnished with the basil sprigs.

Fusilli Lunghi with Sausage & Tomato Sauce

A warming supper dish, perfect for cold winter nights. Save time by using smoked sausages that only need to be reheated. They are sold, singly, in packets in the chiller compartments of supermarkets.

Serves 4
15ml/1 tbsp olive oil
1 medium onion, finely chopped
1 red pepper, seeded and diced
1 green pepper, seeded and diced
2 x 400g/14oz cans
   chopped tomatoes
30ml/2 tbsp tomato purée
10ml/2 tsp mild paprika
450g/1lb/4 cups fusilli lunghi
1 reduced-fat U-shaped smoked
   pork sausage
45ml/3 tbsp chopped
   fresh parsley
salt and freshly ground
   black pepper

1 Heat the oil in a medium saucepan. Add the onion and fry over a medium heat, stirring occasionally, for 5 minutes, until it is beginning to colour.

2 Stir in the peppers, tomatoes, tomato purée and paprika. Bring to the boil, lower the heat and simmer, uncovered, for 15–20 minutes, until the sauce has reduced and thickened.

3 Meanwhile, bring a large pan of water to the boil, add the pasta and cook until it is *al dente*.

4 Heat the U-shaped sausage in a pan of simmering water, following the instructions on the packet. Do not allow the water to boil, as this will cause the skin to split. Alternatively, heat the sausage in the microwave, following the instructions on the packet.

5 Drain the pasta and divide it among four warmed bowls. Drain the sausage, if necessary, remove the outer covering and slice the meat thinly. Add the slices to the sauce, with the parsley, season with salt and pepper to taste and mix well. Top each portion of pasta with sauce and serve immediately.

Tagliatelle with Milanese Sauce

Mushrooms and lean ham in a rich tomato sauce make a tasty topping for tagliatelle.

Serves 4
1 onion, finely chopped
1 celery stick, finely chopped
1 red pepper, seeded and diced
1–2 garlic cloves, crushed
150ml/ ¼ pint/ ⅔ cup
  vegetable stock
400g/14oz can chopped
  tomatoes
15ml/1 tbsp tomato purée
10ml/2 tsp caster sugar
5ml/1 tsp mixed dried herbs
350g/12oz dried tagliatelle,
  preferably mixed colours
115g/4oz/1 ½ cups button
  mushrooms, sliced
60ml/4 tbsp white wine
60ml/4 tbsp lean cooked
  ham, diced
salt and freshly ground
  black pepper
15ml/1 tbsp chopped fresh
  parsley, to garnish

1 Put the chopped onion, celery, pepper and garlic in a non-stick pan. Add the stock, bring to the boil and cook over a medium heat for 5 minutes.

2 Stir in the tomatoes, tomato purée, sugar and dried herbs. Season to taste with salt and pepper. Bring to the boil, then lower the heat and simmer, stirring occasionally, for 30 minutes, until thick.

3 Bring a large pan of lightly salted water to the boil and cook the pasta until it is al dente.

4 Meanwhile, put the mushrooms into a heavy-based pan with the white wine, cover and cook over a medium heat for 3–4 minutes, until the mushrooms are tender and all the wine has been absorbed.

5 Stir the mushrooms into the tomato sauce, then add the diced ham.

6 Drain the pasta well and tip it into a warmed serving dish. Spoon the sauce over, garnish with the chopped parsley and serve immediately.

Home-made Tortellini

When you make your own tortellini, you are in control of the fat content.

Serves 4–6
115g/4oz lean smoked ham
115g/4oz skinless, boneless
  chicken breast
900ml/1 ½ pints/3¾ cups
  vegetable stock
bunch of fresh coriander
30ml/2 tbsp grated Parmesan
  cheese, plus extra for serving
1 egg, beaten, plus egg white
  for brushing
1 quantity Basic Pasta Dough
flour, for dusting
salt and freshly ground
  black pepper

1 Cut the ham and chicken into large chunks and put them into a saucepan with 150ml/ ¼ pint/ ⅔ cup of the stock. Strip the leaves from the coriander. Set some aside for the garnish and chop the rest. Add the stalks to the pan. Bring to the boil, cover and simmer for 20 minutes, until the chicken is tender. Set aside to cool slightly.

2 Drain the ham and chicken, reserving the stock, and mince finely. Put the mixture into a bowl and add the Parmesan, beaten egg and chopped coriander. Season to taste.

3 Roll the pasta into thin sheets, then cut it into 4cm/1 ½in squares. Put 2.5ml/ ½ tsp of filling on each. Brush the edges with egg white and fold each square into a triangle. Press out any air and seal firmly.

4 To make the tortellini, curl each triangle around the tip of a forefinger and press two ends together firmly. Lay the tortellini on a lightly floured dish towel to dry out a little for 30 minutes before cooking.

5 Strain the reserved stock into a large pan and add the remainder. Bring to the boil. Lower the heat slightly and add the tortellini. Cook for 5 minutes. Then turn off the heat, cover the pan and leave to stand for 20–30 minutes. Serve in warmed soup plates with some of the stock. Garnish with the reserved coriander leaves. Serve grated Parmesan separately.

Ham & Spinach Cannelloni

Keep dried cannelloni tubes in the store cupboard, and tasty bakes like this one will be easy to make.

Serves 4
25g/1oz/2 tbsp low-fat spread
½ onion, very finely chopped
175g/6oz/1½ cups frozen chopped spinach, thawed and drained
75g/3oz cooked ham, minced or very finely diced
25g/1oz/ ½ cup fresh white breadcrumbs
115g/4oz/ ½ cup ricotta cheese
75g/3oz/1 cup freshly grated reduced-fat Parmesan cheese
16 dried no-precook cannelloni tubes
salt and freshly ground black pepper

For the white sauce
50g/2oz/ ¼ cup low-fat spread
50g/2oz/ ¼ cup plain flour
900ml/1½ pints/3¾ cups skimmed milk
nutmeg

1 Melt the low-fat spread in a frying pan. Add the onion and fry over a medium heat, stirring occasionally, for 5 minutes, until softened but not browned.

2 Add the spinach and cook for 3 minutes, then tip the mixture into a strainer set over a bowl and press the spinach with the back of a wooden spoon to remove as much liquid as possible. Discard the liquid.

3 Put the spinach mixture into a separate bowl and stir in the ham, breadcrumbs, ricotta and one-third of the grated Parmesan. Season with salt and pepper to taste. Preheat the oven to 190°C/375°F/Gas 5.

4 Make the white sauce. Melt the low-fat spread in a saucepan, add the flour and cook, stirring constantly, for 1–2 minutes. Gradually add the milk, stirring until the sauce boils and thickens. Grate in fresh nutmeg to taste, then season with salt and pepper. Whisk well. Remove the pan from the heat.

5 Spoon a little of the white sauce into an ovenproof dish large enough to hold the cannelloni tubes in a single layer. Fill the cannelloni tubes with the ham and spinach mixture, and place them in the dish. Pour the remaining white sauce over, then sprinkle with the remaining Parmesan.

6 Bake for 35–40 minutes, or until the pasta feels tender when pierced with a skewer. Remove from the oven and allow to stand for 10 minutes before serving.

> **Variations**
> • Use 500g/1¼lb fresh spinach instead of frozen. Discard any stalks and wash the leaves well in cold water. Transfer to a saucepan with just the water clinging to the leaves. Cook over a medium heat for 2–3 minutes, until wilted. Turn into a colander and press out as much liquid as possible. Chop finely and add to the onions.
> • You can also use fresh Swiss chard, which has a similar flavour and can be prepared in exactly the same way.

Pipe Rigate with Peas & Ham

Prettily flecked with pink and green, this is a lovely dish for an informal spring or summer supper party.

Serves 4
350g/12oz/3 cups dried pipe rigate or other pasta shapes
15g/½oz/1 tbsp butter
15ml/1 tbsp olive oil
150–175g/5–6oz/1¼–1½ cups frozen peas, thawed
1 garlic clove, crushed
150ml/ ¼ pint/ ⅔ cup chicken stock
30ml/2 tbsp chopped fresh flat leaf parsley
175ml/6fl oz/ ¾ cup low-fat crème fraîche
115g/4oz prosciutto crudo, shredded
salt and freshly ground black pepper
chopped fresh herbs, such as flat leaf parsley, basil and marjoram, to garnish

1 Bring a large pan of lightly salted water to the boil and cook the pasta until it is *al dente*.

2 Meanwhile, melt half the butter with the olive oil in a separate pan. Add the peas, garlic and stock. Sprinkle in the chopped parsley and season with salt and pepper to taste. Cook over a medium heat, stirring frequently, for 5–8 minutes, or until most of the liquid has been absorbed.

3 Add about half the crème fraîche, increase the heat to high and let the cream bubble, stirring constantly, until it thickens and coats all the peas. Remove from the heat, stir in the prosciutto and taste for seasoning.

4 Tip the cooked pasta into a colander and drain it well. Immediately add the remaining butter to the pasta pan. When it has melted, add the remaining crème fraîche and heat until it is just bubbling.

5 Add the pasta and toss over a medium heat until it is evenly coated. Pour in the pea and ham sauce, toss lightly and heat through. Spoon into warmed bowls and serve immediately, sprinkled with fresh herbs.

Macaroni with Ham & Prawns

A distant relation of Surf 'n' Turf, this supper dish tastes truly delicious.

Serves 4
350g/12oz/3 cups short-
    cut macaroni
30ml/2 tbsp olive oil
175g/6oz smoked ham, diced
12 raw king prawns, peeled
    and deveined
1 garlic clove, chopped

150ml/ ¼ pint/ ⅔ cup red wine
½ small head of
    radicchio, shredded
2 egg yolks, beaten
30ml/2 tbsp chopped fresh flat
    leaf parsley
150ml/ ¼ pint/ ⅔ cup
    low-fat crème fraîche
salt and freshly ground
    black pepper
shredded fresh basil, to garnish

1 Bring a large pan of salted water to the boil and cook the pasta until it is *al dente*.

2 Meanwhile, heat the oil in a frying pan and cook the ham, prawns and garlic for about 5 minutes, stirring occasionally until the prawns have turned pink. Remove the prawns with a slotted spoon.

3 Add the wine and radicchio to the ham mixture, bring to the boil and boil rapidly until the juices are reduced by half.

4 Stir in the egg yolks, parsley and crème fraîche, and simmer until the sauce thickens slightly. Return the prawns to the sauce and season to taste.

5 Drain the pasta and return it to the clean pan. Add the sauce and toss to coat. Serve, garnished with shredded fresh basil.

Cook's Tip
Flat leaf parsley is a pretty herb with more flavour than the curly variety. If you buy a large bunch, finely chop the leftover parsley and freeze it in a small plastic bag. It will then be ready to sprinkle on to bubbling soups or casseroles as a garnish.

Pasta with Spinach, Bacon & Mushrooms

Spinach and bacon are often teamed together. Mushrooms complete the trio in this American recipe.

Serves 4
6 rindless streaky bacon rashers,
    cut in small pieces
1 shallot, finely chopped
225g/8oz/3 cups small
    mushrooms, quartered

450g/1lb fresh spinach leaves,
    coarse stems removed
1.5ml/ ¼ tsp freshly
    grated nutmeg
350g/12oz/3 cups
    dried conchiglie
salt and freshly ground
    black pepper
freshly grated Parmesan cheese,
    to serve (optional)

1 Heat the bacon gently in a frying pan until the fat runs, then raise the heat and cook the bacon until it is crisp. Drain it on kitchen paper, then put it in a bowl.

2 Add the shallot to the bacon fat in the pan and cook for about 5 minutes, until softened.

3 Add the mushrooms and cook until lightly browned, stirring frequently. With a slotted spoon, add the shallot and mushrooms to the bacon.

4 Pour off most of the bacon fat from the pan, add the spinach and cook over a medium heat until wilted, stirring constantly. Sprinkle with the nutmeg, then cook over a high heat until the excess liquid from the spinach has evaporated.

5 Transfer the spinach to a board and chop it coarsely. Return it to the pan. Add the bacon mixture and stir well. Season with salt and pepper and keep warm.

6 Bring a large pan of lightly salted water to the boil and cook the pasta until it is *al dente*. Drain it well and return it to the clean pan. Add the spinach mixture and toss well. Serve in warmed bowls, sprinkled with Parmesan, if using.

Ham-filled Paprika Ravioli

Use a ravioli tray to shape these tasty supper treats.

Serves 4
225g/8oz cooked smoked ham
60ml/4 tbsp mango chutney
1 quantity of Basic Pasta Dough,
   with 5ml/1 tsp ground
   paprika added
egg white, beaten
flour, for dusting
1–2 garlic cloves, crushed

1 celery stick, sliced
2–3 sun-dried tomatoes
1 fresh red chilli, seeded
   and chopped
150ml/ $^{1}/_{4}$ pint/ $^{2}/_{3}$ cup red wine
400g/14oz can
   chopped tomatoes
5ml/1 tsp chopped fresh thyme,
   plus extra to garnish
10ml/2 tsp caster sugar
salt and freshly ground
   black pepper

1 Remove all traces of fat from the ham, place it with the mango chutney in a food processor or blender and mince the mixture finely.

2 Roll the pasta into very thin sheets and lay one piece over a ravioli tray, fitting it carefully into the depressions. Put a teaspoonful of the ham filling into each of the depressions. Brush around the edges of each ravioli with egg white. Cover with another sheet of pasta and press the edges well together to seal.

3 Using a rolling pin, roll over the top of the dough to cut and seal each pocket. Transfer the ravioli to a floured dish towel and leave to rest for 1 hour before cooking.

4 Put the garlic, celery, sun-dried tomatoes, chilli, wine, canned tomatoes and thyme into a pan. Bring to the boil, lower the heat, cover and simmer for 15–20 minutes. Season with salt, pepper and sugar.

5 Bring a large pan of lightly salted water to the boil and cook the ravioli, in batches if necessary, for 4–5 minutes. Drain thoroughly. Spoon a little of the sauce on to each of four warmed serving plates and arrange the ravioli on top. Sprinkle with fresh thyme and serve at once.

Low-fat Cannelloni

A few simple changes make this version of cannelloni the healthier choice.

Serves 4
2 garlic cloves, crushed
2 x 400g/14oz cans
   chopped tomatoes
10ml/2 tsp soft light brown sugar
15ml/1 tbsp shredded fresh basil
15ml/1 tbsp chopped
   fresh marjoram
12–16 dried cannelloni tubes
50g/2oz low-fat mozzarella
   cheese, diced
25g/1oz/ $^{1}/_{4}$ cup grated mature
   Cheddar cheese

25g/1oz/ $^{1}/_{2}$ cup fresh
   white breadcrumbs
salt and freshly ground
   black pepper
fresh flat leaf parsley, to garnish

For the filling
450g/1lb frozen chopped spinach
large pinch of freshly
   grated nutmeg
115g/4oz cooked lean ham, very
   finely chopped
200g/7oz/ scant 1 cup low-fat
   cottage cheese

1 Put the garlic, canned tomatoes, sugar and herbs into a pan, bring to the boil and cook, uncovered, for 30 minutes, stirring occasionally, until fairly thick.

2 Make the filling. Put the spinach into a pan, cover and cook slowly until thawed. Break up with a fork, then increase the heat to drive off any water. Season with salt, pepper and nutmeg. Spoon the spinach into a bowl, let it cool slightly, then add the chopped ham and cottage cheese.

3 Preheat the oven to 180°C/350°F/Gas 4. Pipe or spoon the filling into each tube of uncooked cannelloni.

4 Spoon half the tomato sauce into the base of an ovenproof dish. Arrange the cannelloni in a single layer on top. Scatter over the mozzarella and cover with the rest of the sauce.

5 Sprinkle over the Cheddar cheese and breadcrumbs. Bake for 30–40 minutes, browning the top under a hot grill if necessary. Garnish with the parsley and serve.

Pasta with Devilled Kidneys

The spicy, savoury flavour of the kidneys goes particularly well with tender tagliatelle.

Serves 4
8–10 lamb's kidneys
15ml/1 tbsp sunflower oil
15g/½oz/1 tbsp butter
10ml/2 tsp paprika
5–10ml/1–2 tsp mild
    wholegrain mustard
350g/12oz fresh tagliatelle
salt
chopped fresh parsley, to garnish

1 Bring a large pan of lightly salted water to the boil. Cut the kidneys in half and neatly cut out the white cores with scissors.

2 Heat the oil and butter together in a frying pan. Add the kidneys and cook, turning frequently, for about 2 minutes.

3 In a cup, mix the paprika and mustard with a little salt. Stir the mixture into the pan and continue to cook the kidneys, basting them frequently, for 3–4 minutes.

4 Meanwhile, bring a large pan of lightly salted water to the boil and cook the pasta until *al dente*, then drain thoroughly and divide among warmed bowls. Top with the kidneys, garnish with the parsley and serve.

Pasta with Devilled Liver

Cook as for Pasta with Devilled Kidneys, but use 450g/1lb lamb's liver.
1 Trim the liver, removing any skin, and slice it into strips. Toss these in flour, seasoned with plenty of salt and pepper.
2 Use twice as much oil and butter as for the kidneys. Fry the floured liver strips, then stir in the paprika and mustard. Add a generous dash of Tabasco sauce, if you like. Cook for 3–4 minutes, basting the liver frequently.
3 Serve with the fresh tagliatelle, garnished with chopped parsley.

Spaghetti with Meatballs

Meatballs are fun to make and delicious to eat. This is real hands-on cooking!

Serves 4
350g/12oz dried spaghetti
4 fresh rosemary sprigs, to garnish
freshly grated Parmesan
   cheese, to serve (optional)

For the meatballs
1 onion, chopped
1 garlic clove, chopped
350g/12oz minced lamb
1 egg yolk
15ml/1 tbsp dried mixed herbs
salt and freshly ground
    black pepper
15ml/1 tbsp olive oil

For the sauce
300ml/½ pint/1¼ cups passata
30ml/2 tbsp chopped fresh basil
1 garlic clove, chopped

1 Start by making the meatballs. Put the onion, garlic, minced lamb, egg yolk and mixed herbs in a bowl and season to taste with salt and pepper. Mix together thoroughly, using a spoon at first, then your hands.

2 Divide the mixture into 20 equal-size pieces and mould into balls. Place on a baking sheet, cover with clear film and chill for about 30 minutes.

3 Heat the oil in a large, heavy-based frying pan. Add the meatballs and fry over a medium heat, turning occasionally, for about 10 minutes, until browned all over.

4 Add all the sauce ingredients and bring to the boil. Cover, lower the heat and simmer for about 20 minutes, until the meatballs are tender.

5 Bring a large pan of lightly salted water to the boil and cook the pasta until it is *al dente*.

6 Drain the pasta thoroughly and divide it among four warmed serving plates. Spoon over the meatballs and some of the sauce. Garnish each portion with a fresh rosemary sprig and serve immediately with Parmesan, if using.

Spirali with Rich Meat Sauce

The sauce definitely improves if kept overnight in the fridge. This allows the flavours time enough to mature. There isn't any wine in this meat sauce, but the bacon and redcurrant jelly give it a fine flavour.

Serves 4

15ml/1 tbsp vegetable oil
450g/1lb lean minced beef
115g/4oz rindless lean smoked streaky bacon rashers, chopped
1 onion, chopped
2 celery sticks, chopped
150ml/ ¼ pint/ ⅔ cup chicken stock
45ml/3 tbsp tomato purée
1 garlic clove, chopped
45ml/3 tbsp chopped fresh mixed herbs
15ml/1 tbsp redcurrant jelly
350g/12oz/3 cups dried spirali
salt and freshly ground black pepper
chopped fresh oregano, to garnish

1 Heat the oil in a large saucepan. Add the beef and bacon, and cook over a moderate heat, stirring occasionally, for about 10 minutes, until browned.

2 Add the onion and celery, and cook for 5 minutes, stirring occasionally, then tip the contents of the pan into a metal colander and drain off the excess fat. Return the meat mixture to the pan.

3 Stir in the stock, tomato purée, garlic, herbs and redcurrant jelly. Season well, bring to the boil, then lower the heat, cover and simmer for at least 30 minutes, stirring occasionally.

4 Bring a large pan of lightly salted water to the boil and cook the pasta until it is *al dente*. Drain thoroughly and turn it into a large serving bowl. Pour over the sauce and toss to coat. Serve immediately, garnished with chopped fresh oregano.

> **Variation**
> *You can use sweet mint jelly or chutney instead of the redcurrant jelly.*

Bogus Bolognese

This doesn't pretend to be anything like the real thing, but Worcestershire sauce, chilli and spicy pork sausages ensure that it is full of flavour and makes a very good family meal.

Serves 4

15ml/1 tbsp vegetable oil
1 onion, chopped
225g/8oz lean minced beef
5ml/1 tsp mild chilli powder
15ml/1 tbsp Worcestershire sauce
30ml/2 tbsp plain flour
150ml/ ¼ pint/ ⅔ cup beef stock
4 reduced-fat spicy sausages, sliced
200g/7oz can chopped tomatoes
50g/2oz/ ⅓ cup baby sweetcorn cobs, halved lengthways
15ml/1 tbsp chopped fresh basil
350g/12oz dried spaghetti
salt and freshly ground black pepper
fresh basil sprigs, to garnish

1 Heat the oil in a large saucepan. Add the onion and minced beef, and fry over a moderate heat for 5 minutes, stirring to break up any lumps.

2 Add the chilli powder and cook, stirring constantly, for a further 3 minutes.

3 Stir in the Worcestershire sauce and flour. Cook for 1 minute, stirring constantly, then gradually pour in the stock, stirring constantly. Stir in the sliced sausages, tomatoes, baby sweetcorn and chopped basil. Season with salt and pepper to taste, and bring to the boil. Lower the heat and simmer for 30 minutes.

4 Bring a large pan of lightly salted water to the boil and cook the pasta until it is *al dente*.

5 Drain, place on four individual plates and top with the meat sauce. Garnish with the basil sprigs.

> **Cook's Tip**
> *Make up the bogus Bolognese sauce and freeze in conveniently sized portions for up to two months.*

Low-fat Spaghetti Bolognese

Mushrooms are a gift to the health-conscious cook, as long as they are cooked in wine and not fat.

Serves 8
1 medium onion, chopped
2–3 garlic cloves, crushed
300ml/ ½ pint/1 ¼ cups defatted
    beef or chicken stock
450g/1lb minced turkey or extra
    lean beef
2 x 400g/14oz cans
    chopped tomatoes
5ml/1 tsp dried basil
5ml/1 tsp dried oregano
60ml/4 tbsp tomato purée
450g/1lb/6 cups button
    mushrooms, sliced
150ml/ ¼ pint/ ⅔ cup red wine
450g/1lb dried spaghetti
salt and freshly ground
    black pepper

1 Put the chopped onion and crushed garlic in a pan and pour in half of the stock. Bring to the boil and cook for 5 minutes, until the onion is tender and very little stock remains.

2 Add the turkey or beef and cook over a medium heat for 5 minutes, breaking up any lumps with a fork.

3 Stir in the chopped tomatoes, herbs, remaining beef or chicken stock and tomato purée, and bring to the boil. Lower the heat, cover and simmer for about 1 hour.

4 Meanwhile, put the button mushrooms into a non-stick frying pan with the wine, bring to the boil and cook for 5 minutes, or until the wine has been absorbed. Add the cooked mushrooms to the meat sauce and season to taste with salt and freshly ground black pepper. Keep the sauce hot while you cook the pasta.

5 Bring a large pan of lightly salted water to the boil and cook the spaghetti until it is *al dente*. Drain thoroughly. Transfer to individual warmed plates, top with the meat sauce and serve.

Chilli Mince & Pipe Rigate

Cheer up a chilly evening with this hearty, warming and colourful dish.

Serves 6
450g/1lb extra lean minced beef
1 onion, finely chopped
2–3 garlic cloves, crushed
1–2 fresh red chillies, seeded and
    finely chopped
400g/14oz can
    chopped tomatoes
45ml/3 tbsp tomato purée
5ml/1 tsp mixed dried herbs
450ml/ ¾ pint/1 ¾ cups water
450g/1lb/4 cups dried pipe rigate
400g/14oz can red kidney
    beans, drained
salt and freshly ground
    black pepper

1 Dry-fry the minced beef in a heavy-based non-stick saucepan over a medium heat, breaking up any lumps with a wooden spoon, until browned all over. Drain off any fat that has run from the meat.

2 Add the onion, garlic and chillies, and lower the heat. Cover and cook gently, stirring occasionally, for 5 minutes.

3 Stir in the tomatoes, tomato purée, herbs, and measured water. Bring to the boil, then lower the heat and simmer for 1 ½ hours. Season to taste with salt and pepper and set aside to cool slightly.

4 Bring a large pan of lightly salted water to the boil and cook the pasta until it is *al dente*.

5 Meanwhile, stir the kidney beans into the meat sauce and heat through, stirring occasionally, for about 10 minutes.

6 Drain the pasta and arrange it on warmed plates. Pile the sauce in the centre and serve immediately.

Cook's Tip
If you make the sauce the day before, it will be even more flavoursome and you can also skim off any residual fat.

Meatballs with Cream Sauce

Three types of meat make these meatballs extra special.

Serves 6

25g/ oz/2 tbsp low-fat spread
½ onion, finely chopped
225g/8oz lean minced beef
115g/4oz lean minced veal
225g/8oz lean minced pork
I egg
115g/4oz cooked
  mashed potatoes
30ml/2 tbsp chopped fresh dill
I garlic clove, finely chopped

2.5ml/½ tsp ground allspice
1.5ml/¼ tsp grated nutmeg
40g/1½ oz/ ¾ cup fresh white
  breadcrumbs, soaked in 175ml/
  6fl oz/ ¾ cup skimmed milk
about 40g/1½ oz/ ⅓ cup
  plain flour
30ml/2 tbsp olive oil
450g/1lb dried tagliatelli
125ml/4fl oz/ ½ cup reduced-fat
  single cream
salt and freshly ground
  black pepper
fresh dill sprigs, to garnish

1 Melt half the low-fat spread in a pan and cook the onion over a low heat, until softened. Transfer the onion to a bowl, using a slotted spoon.

2 Add the minced meats, egg, mashed potatoes, dill, garlic, spices and seasoning to the bowl. Add the soaked breadcrumbs and mix well.

3 Shape the mixture into balls about 2.5cm/1in in diameter. Coat them lightly in flour. Heat the oil in a large frying pan and cook the meatballs for 8–10 minutes, until brown on all sides, shaking the pan occasionally.

4 Meanwhile, bring a large pan of lightly salted water to the boil and cook the pasta until it is *al dente*.

5 Using a slotted spoon, transfer the meatballs to a dish and keep them hot. Stir 15ml/1 tbsp flour into the fat in the frying pan. Whisk in the cream, then simmer for 3–4 minutes.

6 Drain the pasta and toss it with the remaining low-fat spread. Divide among six warmed plates, top each with a portion of meatballs and sauce. Garnish with dill and serve immediately.

Pasta Timbales

An alternative way to serve pasta for a special occasion. Mixed with minced beef and tomato, and baked in a lettuce parcel, it makes an impressive dish.

Serves 4

8 cos lettuce leaves
fresh basil sprigs, to garnish

For the filling
15ml/1 tbsp vegetable oil
175g/6oz minced beef

15ml/1 tbsp tomato purée
I garlic clove, crushed
115g/4oz/1 cup dried short-
  cut macaroni
salt and freshly ground
  black pepper

For the sauce
25g/1oz/2 tbsp low-fat spread
25g/1oz/ ¼ cup plain flour
250ml/8fl oz/1 cup low-fat
  crème fraîche
30ml/2 tbsp chopped fresh basil

1 Preheat the oven to 180°C/350°F/Gas 4. Make the filling. Heat the oil in a large pan and fry the beef for 7 minutes. Add the tomato purée and garlic, and cook for 5 minutes.

2 Meanwhile, bring a large pan of lightly salted water to the boil and cook the macaroni until it is *al dente*. Drain the macaroni and stir it into the meat sauce.

3 Line four 150ml/ ¼ pint/ ⅔ cup ramekins with the cos lettuce leaves, overlapping the sides. Season the meat mixture and spoon it into the lettuce-lined ramekins. Fold the lettuce leaves over the filling. Stand the ramekins in a roasting tin and pour in boiling water to come halfway up the sides. Cover the tin with foil and cook in the oven for 20 minutes.

4 While the timbales are cooking, make the sauce. Melt the low-fat spread in a pan. Add the flour and cook, stirring constantly, for 1 minute. Gradually add the crème fraîche, stirring until the sauce boils and thickens. Stir in the basil, with salt and pepper to taste.

5 Turn out the timbales on to warmed plates and pour the sauce around them. Garnish with the basil sprigs and serve.

Special Chow Mein

This famous dish can be as simple or as elaborate as you like. This is a particularly luxurious version.

Serves 6
450g/1lb dried egg noodles
20ml/4 tsp vegetable oil
2 garlic cloves, sliced
5ml/1 tsp chopped fresh
    root ginger
2 fresh red chillies, chopped
2 lap cheong sausages, rinsed
    and sliced
1 skinless, boneless chicken
    breast, thinly sliced
16 raw tiger prawns, peeled, tails
    left intact, and deveined
115g/4oz green beans
225g/8oz/4 cups beansprouts
50g/2oz/1 cup garlic chives
30ml/2 tbsp soy sauce
15ml/1 tbsp oyster sauce
salt and freshly ground
    black pepper
shredded spring onions and fresh
    coriander leaves, to garnish

1 Bring a large pan of lightly salted water to the boil and cook the noodles until they are just tender, checking the packet for information on timing. Drain, rinse under cold water and drain thoroughly again.

2 Preheat a wok and swirl in half the oil. When it is hot, add the garlic, ginger and chillies, and stir-fry over a medium heat for 1 minute.

3 Add the lap cheong slices, chicken, prawns and beans. Stir-fry for about 2 minutes, or until the chicken is cooked and the prawns have changed colour. Transfer the mixture to a bowl and set aside.

4 Heat the rest of the oil in the wok, add the beansprouts and garlic chives, and stir-fry for 1–2 minutes. Add the noodles, and toss and stir to mix. Stir in the soy sauce and oyster sauce, and season to taste with salt and pepper.

5 Return the prawn mixture to the wok and toss over the heat until well mixed and heated through. Transfer the noodle mixture to warmed bowls, garnish with spring onions and coriander leaves, and serve immediately.

Singapore Rice Vermicelli

A lighter rice vermicelli noodle dish, this time made with ham.

Serves 4
10ml/2 tsp vegetable oil
1 egg, lightly beaten
2 garlic cloves, finely chopped
1 large fresh red or green chilli,
    seeded and finely chopped
15ml/1 tbsp medium
    curry powder
1 red pepper, seeded and
    thinly sliced
1 green pepper, seeded and
    thinly sliced
1 carrot, cut into matchsticks
1.5ml/¼ tsp salt
60ml/4 tbsp vegetable stock
225g/8oz diced rice vermicelli,
    soaked in warm water until soft
115g/4oz cooked peeled prawns,
    thawed if frozen
75g/3oz lean cooked ham, cut
    into 1cm/½ in cubes
15ml/1 tbsp light soy sauce

1 Preheat a wok and swirl in 5ml/1 tsp of the oil. When it is hot, add the egg and scramble until just set. Remove with a slotted spoon and set aside.

2 Heat the remaining oil in the clean wok, add the garlic and chilli, and stir-fry for a few seconds. Add the curry powder. Cook for 1 minute, stirring constantly, then stir in the peppers, carrot sticks, salt and stock.

3 Drain the rice vermicelli thoroughly. Heat the contents of the wok until the stock boils. Add the prawns, ham, scrambled egg, rice vermicelli and soy sauce. Mix thoroughly. Cook, stirring constantly, until all the liquid has been absorbed and the mixture is hot. Serve at once.

Cook's Tip
Curry powder varies in flavour, content and degree of heat from brand to brand. Most contain varying proportions of ground cardamom, chilli, cloves, coriander, cumin, ginger, nutmeg, pepper, tamarind and turmeric. They may also contain ajowan, caraway, fennel and mustard seeds.

Egg Fried Noodles

Yellow bean sauce gives these seafood noodles a savoury flavour.

Serves 4–6

350g/12oz medium-thick dried
    egg noodles
30ml/2 tbsp vegetable oil
4 spring onions, cut into 1cm/
    $^1/_2$ in rounds
juice of 1 lime
15ml/1 tbsp soy sauce
2 garlic cloves, finely chopped
175g/6oz skinless, boneless
    chicken breast, sliced
175g/6oz raw prawns, peeled
    and deveined
175g/6oz squid, cleaned and cut
    into rings
15ml/1 tbsp yellow bean sauce
15ml/1 tbsp Thai fish sauce
15ml/1 tbsp soft light
    brown sugar
1 egg
fresh coriander leaves, to garnish

1 Bring a large pan of lightly salted water to the boil and cook the noodles until they are just tender, checking the packet for information on timing. Drain well.

2 Preheat a wok and swirl in half the oil. When it is hot, stir-fry the spring onions over a medium heat for 2 minutes, then add the drained noodles, with the lime juice and soy sauce. Stir-fry for a further 2–3 minutes. Transfer the mixture to a bowl and keep it hot.

3 Heat the remaining oil in the wok. Add the garlic, chicken, prawns and squid. Stir-fry over a high heat until the chicken and seafood are cooked.

4 Stir in the yellow bean sauce, fish sauce and sugar, then break the egg into the mixture, stirring gently until it sets in threads.

5 Add the noodles, toss lightly to mix, and heat through. Transfer to warmed bowls, garnish with coriander leaves and serve immediately.

Udon Pot

Fast food Japanese-style – it's a simple formula, but a winning one. First-class ingredients simmered in a good stock make a marvellous dish.

Serves 4

1 large carrot, cut into bite-
    size chunks
350g/12oz dried udon noodles
225g/8oz skinless, boneless
    chicken breasts, cut into
    bite-size pieces
8 raw king prawns, peeled
    and deveined
4–6 Chinese cabbage leaves, cut
    into short strips
8 fresh shiitake mushrooms,
    stems removed
50g/2oz/ $^1/_2$ cup mangetouts,
    topped and tailed
1.5 litres/2$^1/_2$ pints/6 cups
    defatted home-made chicken
    stock or instant bonito stock
30ml/2 tbsp mirin
soy sauce, to taste
finely chopped spring onions,
    grated fresh root ginger, lemon
    wedges and extra soy sauce,
    to serve

1 Bring a large pan of lightly salted water to the boil and add the carrot chunks. Blanch for 1 minute, then lift out with a slotted spoon and set aside.

2 Add the noodles to the boiling water and cook until just tender, checking the packet for information on timing. Drain, rinse under cold water and drain again.

3 Spoon the carrot chunks and noodles into a large shallow pan or wok and arrange the chicken, prawns, Chinese cabbage leaves, mushrooms and mangetouts on top.

4 Bring the stock to the boil in a separate saucepan. Add the mirin and soy sauce to taste. Pour the stock over the noodle mixture and bring to the boil. Lower the heat, cover, then simmer over a medium heat for 5–6 minutes, until all the ingredients are cooked and tender.

5 Spoon the noodle mixture into a warmed dish and serve at once with side dishes of chopped spring onions, grated ginger, lemon wedges and a little soy sauce.

Sweet & Sour Chicken Noodles

This all-in-one dish is the busy cook's answer to that perennial question of what to cook for supper when time is short and everyone is hungry.

Serves 4

275g/10oz dried egg noodles
15ml/1 tbsp vegetable oil
3 spring onions, chopped
1 garlic clove, crushed
2.5cm/1in piece of fresh root
ginger, grated
5ml/1 tsp hot paprika

5ml/1 tsp ground coriander
3 skinless, boneless chicken
breasts, sliced
115g/4oz/1 cup sugar snap peas,
topped and tailed
115g/4oz/2/3 cup baby sweetcorn
cobs, halved
225g/8oz/4 cups fresh
beansprouts, rinsed
15ml/1 tbsp cornflour
45ml/3 tbsp soy sauce
45ml/3 tbsp lemon juice
15ml/1 tbsp granulated sugar
45ml/3 tbsp chopped fresh
coriander, to garnish

1 Bring a large saucepan of lightly salted water to the boil. Add the noodles. Turn off the heat and leave to stand for 5 minutes. Drain well and reserve.

2 Preheat a wok. Add the oil. When it is hot, stir-fry the spring onions until softened. Stir in the garlic, ginger, paprika, ground coriander and chicken slices. Stir-fry for 3–4 minutes.

3 Add the sugar snap peas, sweetcorn and beansprouts. Toss to mix, then cover and steam for 2–3 minutes, until the sugar snap peas are crisp-tender. Add the noodles and toss over the heat.

4 Stir the cornflour, soy sauce, lemon juice and sugar together in a small bowl. Add to the chicken mixture and simmer briefly to thicken. Serve immediately in heated bowls, garnished with chopped fresh coriander.

Cook's Tip
Light soy sauce has a stronger flavour than the sweeter dark variety, but the latter adds more colour to a dish.

Chicken Chow Mein

Dried egg noodles need very little cooking and are perfect for quick and tasty stir-fried dishes such as this old family favourite.

Serves 4

225g/8oz skinless, boneless
chicken breasts
45ml/3 tbsp soy sauce
15ml/1 tbsp rice wine or
dry sherry
a few drops of dark sesame oil

350g/12oz dried egg noodles
15ml/1 tbsp vegetable oil
2 garlic cloves, finely chopped
50g/2oz/1/2 cup mangetouts,
topped and tailed
115g/4oz/2 cups
beansprouts, rinsed
50g/2oz lean ham,
finely shredded
4 spring onions, finely chopped
salt and freshly ground
black pepper

1 Using a sharp knife, slice the chicken into very fine shreds about 5cm/2in long. Place in a bowl and add 10ml/2 tsp of the soy sauce, with the rice wine or sherry and the sesame oil. Mix well, then set aside.

2 Bring a large pan of lightly salted water to the boil and add the noodles. Turn off the heat and leave to stand for 5 minutes. Drain well and reserve.

3 Preheat a wok and add half the vegetable oil. When it is very hot, add the chicken mixture and stir-fry for 2 minutes, then transfer it to a plate and keep it hot.

4 Wipe the wok clean and heat the remaining oil. Stir in the garlic, mangetouts, beansprouts and shredded ham, and stir-fry for another minute or so. Add the noodles.

5 Toss the noodles over the heat until they are heated through. Add the remaining soy sauce and season with pepper to taste, and salt, if necessary.

6 Return the chicken and any juices to the noodle mixture, add the chopped spring onions and toss the mixture once more. Serve immediately in heated bowls.

Stir-fried Turkey with Broccoli & Mushrooms

This is a really easy, tasty supper dish.

Serves 4

275g/10oz dried egg noodles
115g/4oz/scant 1 cup
  broccoli florets
5ml/1 tsp cornflour
45ml/3 tbsp oyster sauce
15ml/1 tbsp dark soy sauce
120ml/4fl oz/ ½ cup
  chicken stock
10ml/2 tsp lemon juice
30ml/2 tbsp groundnut oil

450g/1lb turkey steaks, cut into
  thin strips
1 small onion, chopped
2 garlic cloves, crushed
10ml/2 tsp grated fresh
  root ginger
115g/4oz/1 ½ cups fresh shiitake
  mushrooms, sliced
4 baby sweetcorn cobs,
  halved lengthways
10ml/2 tsp sesame oil
salt and freshly ground
  black pepper
4 spring onions

1 Bring a large pan of lightly salted water to the boil and add the noodles. Cover, remove from the heat and leave to stand. Divide the broccoli florets into sprigs and thinly slice the stalks diagonally. Finely chop the white parts of the spring onions and thinly shred the green parts.

2 In a bowl, mix together the cornflour, oyster sauce, soy sauce, stock and lemon juice. Set aside.

3 Preheat a wok. Add 15ml/1 tbsp of the groundnut oil. When hot, stir-fry the turkey for 2 minutes, until golden and crispy at the edges. Remove the turkey from the wok and keep it hot.

4 Add the remaining groundnut oil to the wok and stir-fry the onion, garlic and ginger for 1 minute. Increase the heat, add the broccoli, mushrooms and sweetcorn, and stir-fry for 2 minutes.

5 Return the turkey to the wok, then add the sauce with the seasoning. Cook, stirring for 1 minute, until the sauce has thickened. Stir in the sesame oil. Drain the noodles and serve with the stir-fry. Scatter the spring onion on top.

Duck with Noodles, Pineapple & Ginger

As striking as any still-life, but substantially more satisfying for supper.

Serves 2–3

4 spring onions, chopped
2 boneless duck breasts, skinned
15ml/1 tbsp light soy sauce
175g/6oz dried egg noodles
225g/8oz can pineapple rings
75ml/5 tbsp water

4 pieces of drained Chinese stem
  ginger in syrup, plus 45ml/
  3 tbsp syrup from the jar
30ml/2 tbsp cornflour mixed to a
  paste with a little water
175g/6oz each cooked baby
  spinach and blanched
  green beans
¼ each red and green pepper,
  seeded and cut into thin strips
salt and freshly ground black pepper

1 Select a shallow bowl that fits into your steamer and that will accommodate the duck breasts side by side. Spread out the spring onions in the bowl, arrange the duck breasts on top and drizzle the soy sauce over. Cover with non-stick baking paper. Set the steamer over boiling water and cook the duck breasts for about 1 hour, or until tender. Remove the breasts from the steamer and leave to cool slightly.

2 Cut the breasts into thin slices. Place on a plate, moisten with a little of the cooking juices and keep warm. Strain the remaining juices into a small saucepan and set aside.

3 Bring a large pan of lightly salted water to the boil and cook the noodles until they are just tender.

4 Meanwhile, drain the pineapple, reserving 75ml/5 tbsp of the juice. Add this to the reserved cooking juices, with the measured water. Stir in the ginger syrup, then stir in the cornflour paste and cook, stirring until thickened. Season.

5 Cut the pineapple and ginger into attractive shapes. Drain the noodles and swirl them into nest shapes on individual plates. Add the spinach and beans, then the duck. Top with the pineapple, ginger and peppers. Pour over the sauce and serve.

Pork & Noodle Stir-fry

This tasty Chinese dish is both very easy to prepare and healthy.

Serves 4
225g/8oz dried egg noodles
15ml/1 tbsp vegetable oil
1 onion, chopped
1.5cm/ ½in piece of fresh root ginger, chopped
2 garlic cloves, crushed

30ml/2 tbsp soy sauce
60ml/4 tbsp dry white wine
10ml/2 tsp Chinese five-spice powder
450g/1lb lean minced pork
4 spring onions, sliced
50g/2oz/ ¾ cup oyster mushrooms
75g/3oz/ ½ cup drained canned sliced bamboo shoots
sesame oil, to serve (optional)

1 Bring a large pan of lightly salted water to the boil and cook the noodles until they are just tender, checking the packet for timing. Drain, rinse under cold water and drain well again.

2 Preheat a wok and swirl in the oil. When it is hot, add the onion, ginger, garlic, soy sauce and wine. Cook for 1 minute. Stir in the Chinese five-spice powder.

3 Add the pork and cook for 10 minutes, stirring continuously. Add the spring onions, mushrooms and bamboo shoots, and cook for 5 minutes more.

4 Stir in the drained noodles, and toss over the heat until they are heated through and have mixed with the other ingredients. Drizzle over a little sesame oil, if using, and serve immediately.

Indonesian Pork & Noodles

This spicy noodle dish couldn't be easier.

Serves 4
225g/8oz broccoli, divided into florets
225g/8oz egg noodles
15ml/1 tbsp groundnut oil
225g/8oz boneless loin of pork, cut into thin strips
1 carrot, cut into matchsticks

1 onion, finely chopped
2 garlic cloves, crushed
5ml/1 tsp grated fresh root ginger
2.5ml/½ tsp dried shrimp paste
2.5ml/½ tsp sambal oelek
4 Chinese cabbage leaves, shredded
30ml/2 tbsp light soy sauce, plus extra to serve
10ml/2 tsp palm sugar
salt

1 Bring a large pan of lightly salted water to the boil and blanch the broccoli for 1 minute. Remove with a slotted spoon.
2 Bring the water back to the boil and cook the noodles until they are just tender, checking the packet for information on timing. Drain, rinse under cold water and drain well again.
3 Preheat a wok and swirl in the oil. Add the pork, carrot, onion, garlic, ginger, shrimp paste and sambal oelek, and stir-fry over a medium to high heat for 3–4 minutes.
4 Add the broccoli and Chinese cabbage leaves, and stir-fry for 1 minute more.
5 Add the noodles, soy sauce and sugar, and stir-fry for 3–4 minutes, until heated through. Transfer to a warmed serving dish and serve immediately with extra soy sauce.

Lemon Grass Pork

Chillies and lemon grass flavour this simple stir-fry, while peanuts add crunch.

Serves 4
450g/1lb boneless loin of pork
2 lemon grass stalks, trimmed and finely chopped
4 spring onions, thinly sliced
5ml/1 tsp salt
12 black peppercorns, coarsely crushed
15ml/1 tbsp groundnut oil
2 garlic cloves, chopped

2 fresh red chillies, seeded and chopped
225g/8oz dried rice vermicelli, soaked in warm water until soft
5ml/1 tsp light brown soft sugar
30ml/2 tbsp fish sauce
25g/1oz/ ¼ cup roasted unsalted peanuts, chopped
salt and freshly ground black pepper
roughly torn coriander leaves, to garnish

1 Trim any fat from the pork. Cut the meat across into 5mm/ ¼in thick slices, then into 5mm/¼in strips. Put them in a bowl with the lemon grass, spring onions, salt and peppercorns. Mix well, cover and leave to marinate for 30 minutes.

2 Heat a wok and swirl in the oil. When it is hot, stir-fry the pork for 3 minutes. Add the garlic and chillies, and stir-fry for 5–8 minutes more, until the pork no longer looks pink.

3 Meanwhile, bring a large pan of lightly salted water to the boil. Drain the rice vermicelli, add it to the water and cook briefly until just tender. Drain thoroughly and pile on to a warmed serving dish.

4 Add the sugar, fish sauce and peanuts to the pork mixture and toss to mix. Taste and adjust the seasoning, if necessary. Spoon on to the dish, alongside the noodles, garnish with the coriander leaves and serve.

> **Variation**
> Use skinless, boneless chicken breast if you prefer it to pork.

Beef & Broccoli Stir-fry

A quick-to-make dish with Eastern appeal.

Serves 4

10ml/2 tsp cornflour
45ml/3 tbsp soy sauce
45ml/3 tbsp ruby port
15ml/1 tbsp sunflower oil
350g/12oz lean beef steak, cut
   into thin strips
1 garlic clove, crushed
2.5cm/1in piece of fresh root
   ginger, finely chopped
1 red pepper, seeded and sliced
225g/8oz/1½ cups small
   broccoli florets
350g/12oz rice vermicelli, soaked
   in warm water until soft
fresh parsley sprigs, to garnish

1 Mix the cornflour, soy sauce and port in a small bowl.

2 Preheat a wok. Add the oil. When hot, stir-fry the beef, garlic and ginger until the beef is browned. Add the red pepper and broccoli, and stir-fry for 4–5 minutes, until just tender.

3 Stir the cornflour mixture into the wok. Cook, stirring constantly, until the sauce thickens and becomes glossy. Drain the vermicelli, add it to the wok and toss over the heat for 2–3 minutes until heated through. Serve in warmed bowls, garnished with parsley.

> **Variations**
> *You could use red wine if you do not have port. Try using other vegetables such as mangetouts, sugar snap peas or fresh asparagus instead of the broccoli.*

Rice Noodles with Beef & Black Bean Sauce

This is an excellent combination – beef with a chilli sauce tossed with silky smooth rice noodles.

Serves 4

450g/1lb fresh flat rice noodles
30ml/2 tbsp vegetable oil
1 onion, finely sliced
2 garlic cloves, finely chopped
2 slices of fresh root ginger,
   finely chopped
225g/8oz mixed peppers, seeded
   and cut into strips
350g/12oz lean rump steak,
   finely sliced against the grain
45ml/3 tbsp fermented black
   beans, rinsed in warm water,
   drained and chopped
30ml/2 tbsp soy sauce
30ml/2 tbsp oyster sauce
15ml/1 tbsp chilli black
   bean sauce
15ml/1 tbsp cornflour
120ml/4fl oz/½ cup stock
   or water
salt and freshly ground
   black pepper
2 spring onions, finely chopped,
   and 2 fresh red chillies, seeded
   and finely sliced, to garnish

1 Rinse the noodles under hot water and drain well. Preheat a wok. Add two tablespoons of the oil. When hot, stir-fry the onion, garlic, ginger and mixed pepper strips for 3–5 minutes. Remove with a slotted spoon and keep hot.

2 Add the remaining oil to the wok. When hot, add the sliced beef and fermented black beans, and stir-fry over a high heat for 5 minutes, or until they are cooked.

3 In a small bowl, mix the soy sauce, oyster sauce and chilli black bean sauce with the cornflour and stock or water until smooth. Add the cornflour paste to the beef mixture in the wok, then stir in the onion mixture. Cook over a medium heat, stirring constantly, for 1 minute.

4 Add the noodles and mix lightly. Toss over a medium heat until the noodles are heated through. Adjust the seasoning if necessary. Serve at once, garnished with the chopped spring onions and chillies.

VEGETARIAN PASTA

Eliche with Chargrilled Peppers
Capellini with Peppers & Mangetouts
Tagliatelle with Tomato & Mushroom Sauce
Penne with Broccoli & Chilli
Farfalle with Red Pepper Sauce
Pasta Napoletana
Lasagnette with Tomato & Red Wine Sauce
Wholemeal Pasta with Caraway Cabbage
Tagliatelle & Vegetable Ribbons
Fettuccine with Broccoli & Garlic
Tagliatelle with Broccoli & Spinach
Torchiette with Tossed Vegetables
Pasta with Tomato Sauce & Roasted Vegetables
Pasta with Low-fat Pesto Sauce
Farfalle with Grilled Pepper Sauce
Tagliatelle with Sun-dried Tomatoes
Ratatouille Penne
Pasta with Roasted Pepper & Tomato Sauce
Tagliatelle with "Hit-the-pan" Salsa
Tagliatelle with Pea Sauce, Asparagus & Broad Beans
Chinese Ribbons
Low-fat Tagliatelle with Mushrooms
Tagliatelle with Spinach Gnocchi
Spinach & Hazelnut Lasagne
Aubergine & Mixed Vegetable Lasagne
Pappardelle & Provençal Sauce
Sweet & Sour Peppers with Farfalle
Spinach Ravioli Crescents
Vegetarian Cannelloni
Spaghetti with Mixed Bean Chilli
Stir-fried Noodles with Beansprouts
Five-spice Vegetable Noodles
Beancurd Stir-fry with Egg Noodles
Noodles Primavera
Oriental Vegetable Noodles
Spicy Vegetable Chow Mein
Chow Mein with Cashew Nuts

Eliche with Chargrilled Peppers

This is a dish for high summer when peppers and tomatoes ripen naturally and are plentiful. It is equally good cold as a salad.

Serves 4
3 large peppers (red, yellow and orange)
350g/12oz/3 cups fresh or dried eliche
1–2 garlic cloves, finely chopped
4 ripe Italian plum tomatoes, peeled, seeded and diced
50g/2oz/ ½ cup stoned black olives, halved or quartered lengthways
60ml/4 tbsp extra virgin olive oil
a handful of fresh basil leaves
salt and freshly ground black pepper

1 Preheat the grill. Cut the peppers in half, remove the cores and seeds, and place them cut side down in the grill pan. Grill until the skins have blistered and begun to char.

2 Put the peppers in a bowl, cover with several layers of kitchen paper and set aside for 10 minutes.

3 Bring a large pan of lightly salted water to the boil and cook the pasta until it is *al dente*.

4 While the pasta is cooking, peel the peppers, slice the flesh thinly and place it in a large bowl.

5 Add the garlic, tomatoes, olives and olive oil to the peppers. Mix lightly, then add salt and pepper to taste.

6 Drain the cooked pasta and tip it into the bowl. Add the basil leaves. Toss thoroughly to mix and serve immediately in warmed bowls.

Variation
A few strips of sun-dried tomatoes would give this even more flavour. Choose the type in oil, and use some of the oil in the dressing, if you like.

Capellini with Peppers & Mangetouts

The vegetables in this pretty, summery dish are barely cooked – rather, they are just heated through. As a result, they stay lovely and crisp, providing a contrast to the tender pasta.

Serves 4
350g/12oz dried capellini
10ml/2 tsp groundnut oil
30ml/2 tbsp cornflour
30ml/2 tbsp water
10ml/2 tsp vegetable oil
3 garlic cloves, finely chopped
175ml/6fl oz/ ¾ cup vegetable stock
45ml/3 tbsp dry sherry
15ml/1 tbsp sesame oil
15ml/1 tbsp light soy sauce
5ml/1 tsp chilli sauce
2.5ml/ ½ tsp caster sugar
2.5ml/ ½ tsp Szechuan peppercorns, crushed
1 red pepper, seeded and cut into strips
1 yellow pepper, seeded and cut into strips
115g/4oz mangetouts, trimmed and halved
10 button mushrooms, thinly sliced
3 spring onions
pared rind of 1 orange, thinly shredded, to garnish

1 Bring a large pan of lightly salted water to the boil and cook the pasta until it is *al dente*. Drain in a colander, then transfer to a large bowl and stir in the groundnut oil.

2 Put the cornflour in a small bowl and stir in the measured water to make a smooth paste.

3 Preheat a wok or large, heavy-based frying pan and add the vegetable oil. When it is hot, add the garlic and stir-fry for about 20 seconds. Add the vegetable stock, sherry, sesame oil, soy sauce, chilli sauce, sugar and Szechuan peppercorns. Bring to the boil, stirring constantly. Pour in the cornflour mixture, stirring all the time until slightly thickened.

4 Add the pasta and vegetables to the wok. Toss over the heat for about 2 minutes, or until the mixture is hot. Serve at once, garnished with the orange rind.

Tagliatelle with Tomato & Mushroom Sauce

Using dried mushrooms gives extra concentrated flavour to the sauce.

Serves 4
25g/1oz/ ½ cup dried Italian
   mushrooms (porcini)
175ml/6fl oz/ ¾ cup hot water
900g/2lb tomatoes, peeled,
   seeded and chopped
1.5ml/ ¼ tsp dried hot
   chilli flakes

1 large garlic clove, finely chopped
350g/12oz dried tagliatelle
   or fettuccine
5ml/1 tsp olive oil
salt and freshly ground
   black pepper
freshly grated strong hard cheese,
   to serve

1 Put the dried mushrooms in a bowl and pour over the hot water to cover. Leave to soak for 20 minutes.

2 Meanwhile, put the tomatoes in a saucepan and add the chilli flakes. Bring to the boil, lower the heat and simmer, stirring occasionally, for 30–40 minutes, or until thick.

3 When the mushrooms have finished soaking, lift them out and squeeze them over the bowl. Set them aside. Carefully pour the soaking liquid into the tomatoes through a muslin-lined strainer, leaving any sandy grit in the base of the bowl. Simmer the tomato sauce for 15 minutes more.

4 Meanwhile dry-fry the garlic and mushrooms in a non-stick frying pan for 3 minutes, stirring. Add to the tomato sauce and mix well. Season with salt and pepper, and keep hot.

5 Bring a large pan of lightly salted water to the boil and cook the pasta until it is *al dente*. Drain it well and return it to the pan. Toss with the oil. Divide among warmed plates, spoon the sauce on top and serve with strong hard cheese.

Penne with Broccoli & Chilli

Chunky, with just enough "bite" to provide an interesting contrast to the broccoli, penne are perfect in this easy dish.

Serves 4
350g/12oz/3 cups dried penne
450g/1lb/generous 3 cups small
   broccoli florets

30ml/2 tbsp vegetable stock
1 garlic clove, crushed
1 small fresh red chilli, sliced, or
   2.5ml/ ½ tsp chilli sauce
60ml/4 tbsp low-fat
   natural yogurt
30ml/2 tbsp toasted pine nuts
   or cashews
salt and freshly ground
   black pepper

1 Bring a pan of lightly salted water to the boil and add the pasta. When the water returns to the boil, place the broccoli in a steamer basket set over the top. Cover and cook for 8–10 minutes, until both the pasta and the broccoli are just tender.

2 When the pasta is almost ready, heat the stock in a separate pan, and add the garlic and chilli or chilli sauce. Stir over a low heat for 2–3 minutes.

3 Drain the pasta and stir it into the flavoured stock, with the broccoli and yogurt. Season to taste with salt and pepper, tip into a warmed serving bowl and sprinkle with the toasted nuts. Serve immediately.

Variations
• *You could substitute green Tabasco sauce for the chilli if you like a "kick" of spice, but prefer something a little milder.*
• *For a slightly richer taste, you could use smetana instead of low-fat yogurt.*

Farfalle with Red Pepper Sauce

A quick and easy sauce that tastes great with pasta.

Serves 4
450g/1lb/4 cups dried farfalle
2 large red peppers, seeded and
   finely diced
1 garlic clove, crushed

3 ripe tomatoes, peeled, seeded
   and chopped
120ml/4fl oz/ ½ cup
   vegetable stock
5ml/1 tsp balsamic vinegar
salt and freshly ground
   black pepper
chopped fresh herbs, to garnish

1 Bring a large pan of lightly salted water to the boil and cook the pasta until it is *al dente*.
2 Meanwhile, make the sauce. Set about 45ml/3 tbsp of the diced red pepper aside for the garnish. Put the rest in a pan with the garlic, tomatoes and stock. Bring to the boil, then lower the heat and simmer, stirring occasionally, until the mixture is thick. Stir in the balsamic vinegar and season to taste.
3 Drain the pasta, tip it into a warmed bowl and toss with the red pepper sauce. Garnish with the reserved red pepper and chopped herbs, and serve.

Pasta Napoletana

Classic cooked tomato sauce makes a healthy choice, when it is served with pasta and not too much cheese.

Serves 4
900g/2lb fresh ripe red tomatoes
1 medium onion, chopped
1 medium carrot, diced
1 celery stick, diced
150ml/ ¼ pint/ ⅔ cup dry
   white wine
1 fresh parsley sprig
a pinch of caster sugar
15ml/1 tbsp chopped
   fresh oregano
450g/1lb/4 cups pappardelle
   or lasagnette
salt and freshly ground
   black pepper
freshly grated strong hard cheese,
   to serve
fresh basil, to garnish

1 Peel the tomatoes, chop them roughly and put them in a pan. Add the onion, carrot, celery, wine, parsley sprig and sugar, and mix well. Bring to the boil, then lower the heat and simmer, half-covered, for 45 minutes, until very thick, stirring occasionally.

2 Remove and discard the parsley sprig. Transfer the tomato sauce to a blender or food processor and process until smooth, then return it to the clean pan. Stir in the oregano, season to taste with salt and pepper, and heat through gently.

3 Meanwhile, bring a large pan of lightly salted water to the boil and cook the pasta until it is *al dente*.

4 Drain the pasta thoroughly and return it to the clean pan. Add the sauce and toss to mix. Serve in warmed bowls, with grated cheese, garnished with basil.

> **Cook's Tips**
> • Fresh Italian plum tomatoes are best for this sauce, especially if they have been home grown.
> • The sauce can be puréed by rubbing it through a fine strainer with the back of a wooden spoon.

Lasagnette with Tomato & Red Wine Sauce

A classic sauce that is simply delicious served with curly pasta. It needs no extra accompaniments.

Serves 4
15ml/1 tbsp olive oil
1 onion, chopped
30ml/2 tbsp tomato purée
5ml/1 tsp mild paprika
2 x 400g/14oz cans
   chopped tomatoes
pinch of drained oregano
300ml/ ½ pint/1¼ cups dry
   red wine
large pinch of caster sugar
350g/12oz dried lasagnette or
   other long pasta
salt and freshly ground
   black pepper
chopped fresh flat leaf parsley,
   to garnish
shavings of strong hard cheese,
   to serve (optional)

1 Heat the oil in a large, heavy-based frying pan. Add the onion and fry over a low heat, stirring occasionally, for 10 minutes, until softened. Stir in the tomato purée and paprika, and cook for 3 minutes.

2 Add the tomatoes, oregano, wine and sugar, and season with salt and pepper to taste. Bring to the boil, lower the heat and simmer for 20 minutes, until the sauce has reduced and thickened, stirring occasionally.

3 Meanwhile, bring a large pan of lightly salted water to the boil and cook the pasta until it is *al dente*.

4 Drain the pasta, return to the clean pan and toss with the tomato sauce. Serve in warmed bowls, garnished with chopped parsley and with cheese shavings sprinkled on top, if using.

Wholemeal Pasta with Caraway Cabbage

Crunchy cabbage and Brussels sprouts are perfect partners for pasta in this healthy dish. Caraway seeds and cabbage are a classic combination. Not only do their flavours complement each other, but caraway is also an aid to digestion and reduces the odour of cabbage when it is cooking.

Serves 6
3 onions, roughly chopped
400ml/14fl oz/1²/₃ cups
   vegetable stock
350g/12oz round white cabbage,
   roughly chopped
350g/12oz Brussels sprouts,
   trimmed and halved
10ml/2 tsp caraway seeds
15ml/1 tbsp chopped fresh dill
200g/7oz/1³/₄ cups fresh or dried
   wholemeal spirali
salt and freshly ground
   black pepper
fresh dill sprigs, to garnish

1 Put the onions in a large saucepan and add half the stock. Bring to the boil, cover and cook over a low heat for about 10 minutes, stirring often, until the onion has softened and most of the liquid has been absorbed.

2 Add the cabbage and Brussels sprouts, and cook over a high heat, stirring, for 2–3 minutes, then stir in the caraway seeds and chopped dill.

3 Pour in the remaining vegetable stock, and season with salt and pepper to taste. Cover and simmer over a low heat for about 10 minutes, until the cabbage and Brussels sprouts are crisp-tender.

4 Meanwhile, bring a large pan of lightly salted water to the boil and cook the pasta until al dente.

5 Drain the pasta, tip it into a bowl and add the cabbage mixture. Toss lightly, adjust the seasoning and serve immediately, garnished with dill sprigs.

Tagliatelle & Vegetable Ribbons

Courgettes and carrots are cut into thin, delicate ribbons so that when they are cooked and tossed with tagliatelle they look like coloured pasta.

Serves 4
2 large courgettes
2 large carrots
250g/9oz fresh egg tagliatelle
15ml/1 tbsp extra virgin olive oil
flesh of 3 roasted garlic cloves,
   plus extra roasted garlic cloves,
   to serve (optional)
salt and freshly ground
   black pepper

1 With a vegetable peeler, cut the courgettes and carrots into long thin ribbons. Bring a large pan of lightly salted water to the boil and add the courgette and carrot ribbons. Boil for 30 seconds, then lift out the vegetable ribbons with a slotted spoon and set them aside.

2 Add the tagliatelle to the boiling water and cook until it is al dente.

3 Drain the pasta and return it to the pan. Add the vegetable ribbons, oil and garlic, and season with salt and pepper to taste. Toss over a medium to high heat until well mixed. Serve immediately, with extra roasted garlic, if you like.

> **Cook's Tip**
> Roasted garlic has a surprisingly mild and sweet flavour. To roast garlic, put a whole head of garlic on a lightly oiled baking sheet and drizzle a little extra olive oil over it. Place in a preheated 180°C/350°F/Gas 4 oven and roast for about 30–45 minutes. Remove the garlic from the oven and set it aside. When cool enough to handle, dig out the flesh from the cloves with the point of a knife, or simply squeeze the soft flesh from the individual cloves with your fingers. Individual cloves can be roasted in the same way, brushed with a little olive oil and cooked for about 20 minutes.

Fettuccine with Broccoli & Garlic

In this recipe, broccoli is mashed with wine and cheese to make a tasty coating sauce.

Serves 4
3–4 garlic cloves, crushed
350g/12oz/2½ cups
  broccoli florets
150ml/¼ pint/⅔ cup
  vegetable stock
60ml/4 tbsp white wine
30ml/2 tbsp chopped fresh basil
60ml/4 tbsp freshly grated strong
  hard cheese
350g/12oz fresh or dried
  fettuccine or tagliatelle
salt and freshly ground
  black pepper
fresh basil leaves, to garnish

1 Put the garlic, broccoli and stock into a large saucepan. Bring to the boil over a medium heat and cook for 5 minutes, or until the broccoli is tender, stirring from time to time.

2 Mash with a fork or potato masher until the broccoli is roughly chopped. Stir in the white wine, chopped basil and cheese. Season to taste with salt and pepper, and leave over a low heat while you cook the pasta.

3 Bring a large pan of lightly salted water to the boil and cook the fettuccine or tagliatelle until *al dente*.

4 Drain the pasta well and return to the pan. Pour over half the broccoli sauce and toss gently. Divide among warmed plates, top with the remaining broccoli sauce, garnish with the basil leaves and serve immediately.

Cook's Tip
When buying broccoli, look for stems that are neither dry and wrinkled nor woody, with tightly packed, dark green flowerheads. There should be no sign of yellowing. It is best eaten on the day of purchase and cannot be kept, even in a cool dark place, for more than a couple of days without the flowerheads turning yellow.

Tagliatelle with Broccoli & Spinach

This is an excellent vegetarian supper dish. It is nutritious and filling and needs no accompaniment.

Serves 4
2 heads of broccoli
450g/1lb fresh spinach leaves,
  stalks removed
freshly grated nutmeg
450g/1lb fresh or dried
  egg tagliatelle
15ml/1 tbsp extra virgin olive oil
juice of ½ lemon
salt and freshly ground
  black pepper
freshly grated strong hard cheese,
  to serve (optional)

1 Put the broccoli in the basket of a steamer, cover and steam over boiling water for 10 minutes.

2 Add the spinach to the broccoli, cover and steam for 4–5 minutes, or until both the vegetables are tender. Towards the end of the cooking time, sprinkle them with freshly grated nutmeg, and season with salt and pepper to taste. Transfer the vegetables to a colander.

3 Top up the water in the steamer and add salt. Bring to the boil, then cook the pasta until *al dente*. Meanwhile, chop the broccoli and spinach.

4 Drain the pasta. Heat the oil in the pasta pan, add the pasta and chopped vegetables, and toss over a medium heat until evenly mixed. Sprinkle in some of the lemon juice and plenty of black pepper, then taste and add more lemon juice, salt and nutmeg if you like. Serve immediately, sprinkled with freshly grated cheese, if using, and black pepper.

Variations
• To add both texture and protein, garnish the finished dish with 25g/1oz/¼ cup toasted pine nuts.
• Add a sprinkling of dried, crushed red chillies with the black pepper in step 4.

Torchiette with Tossed Vegetables

Cooking the pasta in water flavoured by the vegetables gives it a fresh taste.

Serves 4

225g/8oz thin asparagus spears, trimmed and cut in half
115g/4oz/1 cup mangetouts, topped and tailed
115g/4oz/⅔ cup baby corn cobs
225g/8oz whole baby carrots, trimmed
1 small red pepper, seeded and chopped
8 spring onions, sliced
225g/8oz/2 cups dried torchiette or other pasta shapes
150ml/1/4 pint/⅔ cup low-fat cottage cheese
150ml/¼ pint/⅔ cup low-fat natural yogurt
15ml/1 tbsp lemon juice
15ml/1 tbsp chopped fresh parsley
15ml/1 tbsp snipped chives
skimmed milk (optional)
salt and freshly ground black pepper

1 Bring a large pan of lightly salted water to the boil. Add the asparagus spears and cook for 2 minutes.

2 Add the mangetouts and cook for 2 minutes more. Using a slotted spoon, transfer the vegetables to a colander, rinse them under cold water, drain and set aside.

3 Bring the water in the pan back to the boil, add the corn cobs, carrots, red pepper and spring onions, and cook until tender. Lift out with a slotted spoon. Drain in a colander, then rinse and drain again.

4 Bring the water back to the boil and add the pasta. Cook it until it is *al dente*.

5 Meanwhile, put the cottage cheese, yogurt, lemon juice, parsley and chives into a food processor or blender and process until smooth. Thin the sauce with skimmed milk, if necessary, and season to taste with salt and pepper.

6 Drain the pasta, return it to the clean pan, and add the vegetables and cottage cheese sauce. Toss lightly and serve immediately in warmed bowls.

Pasta with Tomato Sauce & Roasted Vegetables

This scrumptious dish also tastes good cold, and makes great picnic fare.

Serves 4

1 aubergine
2 courgettes
1 large onion
2 peppers, preferably red or yellow, seeded
450g/1lb plum tomatoes
2–3 garlic cloves, roughly chopped
30ml/2 tbsp olive oil
300ml/½ pint/1¼ cups passata
8 black olives, halved and stoned (optional)
350g/12oz/3 cups dried pasta shapes, such as rigatoni or penne
salt and freshly ground black pepper
60ml/4 tbsp shredded fresh basil and four sprigs basil leaves, to garnish

1 Preheat the oven to 240°C/475°F/Gas 9. Cut the aubergine, courgettes, onion, peppers and tomatoes into large chunks. Discard the tomato seeds.

2 Spread out the vegetables in a large roasting tin. Sprinkle the garlic and oil over the vegetables, and stir and turn to mix evenly. Season to taste with salt and pepper.

3 Roast the vegetables for 30 minutes, or until they are soft and have begun to char around the edges. Stir halfway through the cooking time.

4 Scrape the vegetable mixture into a pan. Stir in the passata and olives, if using, and heat gently.

5 Bring a large pan of lightly salted water to the boil and cook the pasta until it is *al dente*.

6 Drain the pasta and return it to the clean pan. Add the sauce and toss to mix well. Serve immediately in a warmed bowl, sprinkled with the shredded basil and garnished with a basil sprig.

Pasta with Low-fat Pesto Sauce

Unlike traditional pesto, which is made with lashings of olive oil, this simple sauce is relatively low in fat but still full of flavour.

Serves 4

225g/8oz/2 cups dried pasta
   shapes, such as fusilli or farfalle
50g/2oz/1 cup fresh basil leaves
25g/1oz/½ cup fresh
   parsley sprigs
1 garlic clove, crushed
25g/1oz/¼ cup pine nuts
115g/4oz/½ cup curd cheese or
   very low-fat fromage frais
30ml/2 tbsp freshly grated strong
   hard cheese
salt and freshly ground
   black pepper
few sprigs of fresh basil,
   to garnish

1 Bring a large pan of lightly salted water to the boil and cook the pasta until *al dente*.

2 Meanwhile, put half the basil and half the parsley into a food processor or blender. Add the garlic, pine nuts and curd cheese or fromage frais, and process until smooth.

3 Add the remaining basil and parsley, with the strong hard cheese, and season with salt and pepper to taste. Process until the herbs are finely chopped.

4 Toss the pasta with the pesto and serve immediately on warmed plates, garnished with fresh basil sprigs.

> **Cook's Tip**
> *Fromage frais is a kind of curd cheese made from skimmed pasteurized cow's milk. Sometimes, it is enriched with cream to give it a firmer texture. However, this also gives it a rather higher fat content of about eight per cent. Look for the softer type that is labelled "virtually fat-free", which has zero fat, or the slightly firmer low-fat fromage frais which contains some fat. Make sure that you do not buy sweetened fromage frais which contains added sugar.*

Farfalle with Grilled Pepper Sauce

This healthy vegetarian dish is packed with vitamin C and full of flavour.

Serves 4

4 peppers, preferably mixed
   colours, halved and seeded
3 plum tomatoes, peeled
   and chopped
1 red onion, thinly sliced
1 garlic clove, thinly sliced
350g/12oz/3 cups dried farfalle
   or other shapes
salt and freshly ground
   black pepper
30ml/2 tbsp grated strong hard
   cheese, to garnish (optional)

1 Preheat the grill. Place the peppers, cut side down, in a grill pan and place under high heat until the skins have blistered and begun to char. Put them in a bowl and cover with several layers of kitchen paper. Set aside for 10–15 minutes.

2 Meanwhile, place the chopped tomatoes, onion and garlic in a heavy-based pan over a low heat. Bring to simmering point, cover and cook gently, stirring occasionally, for about 8–10 minutes, until the onion is tender and the sauce has thickened.

3 Peel the skin from the peppers and slice the flesh thinly. Stir them into the tomato sauce, heat gently, and season with salt and pepper to taste. Leave the pan over a low heat while you cook the pasta.

4 Bring a large pan of lightly salted water to the boil and cook the pasta until *al dente*.

5 Drain the pasta well and transfer to four warmed bowls. Top with the pepper sauce and serve, sprinkled with strong hard cheese, if using.

> **Cook's Tip**
> *Grilling the peppers not only makes them easy to peel, it also imparts a delicious flavour to the flesh, making it sweeter and less acerbic than when it is raw.*

Tagliatelle with Sun-dried Tomatoes

Choose plain sun-dried tomatoes for this sauce, instead of those preserved in oil, as they would increase the fat content.

Serves 4
1 garlic clove, crushed
1 celery stick, finely sliced
115g/4oz/2 cups sun-dried tomatoes, finely chopped
90ml/6 tbsp red wine
8 plum tomatoes
350g/12oz dried tagliatelle
salt and freshly ground black pepper

1 Put the garlic, celery, sun-dried tomatoes and wine into a large saucepan. Cook over a low heat, stirring occasionally, for 15 minutes.

2 Meanwhile, plunge the plum tomatoes into a saucepan of boiling water for 1 minute, then into cold water. Slip off their skins. Cut the tomatoes in half, scoop out the seeds and roughly chop the flesh.

3 Stir the plum tomatoes into the sun-dried tomato mixture, and season to taste with salt and pepper. Leave the pan over a low heat while you cook the pasta.

4 Bring a large pan of lightly salted water to the boil and cook the tagliatelle until it is *al dente*.

5 Drain the pasta well and return to the clean pan. Add half the tomato sauce and toss thoroughly to coat. Divide among warmed individual plates and top with the remaining sauce. Serve immediately.

> **Cook's Tip**
> *This dish looks particularly attractive made with a mixture of plain, spinach-flavoured and tomato-flavoured tagliatelle. It is also delicious with wholemeal pasta.*

Ratatouille Penne

Marinated beancurd adds interest to a popular vegetarian dish.

Serves 6
1 small aubergine
2 courgettes, thickly sliced
200g/7oz firm beancurd (tofu), cubed
45ml/3 tbsp dark soy sauce
1 garlic clove, crushed
20ml/4 tsp sesame seeds
1 small red pepper, seeded and sliced
1 onion, finely chopped
1–2 garlic cloves, crushed
150ml/ ¼ pint/ ⅔ cup vegetable stock
3 firm ripe tomatoes, peeled, seeded and quartered
15ml/1 tbsp chopped fresh mixed herbs
225g/8oz/2 cups dried penne
salt and freshly ground black pepper

1 Cut the aubergine into 2.5cm/1in cubes. Put these into a colander with the courgettes, sprinkle with salt and leave over the sink to drain for 30 minutes.

2 Put the beancurd in a bowl and add the soy sauce, garlic and half the sesame seeds. Stir, cover and marinate for 30 minutes.

3 Put the pepper, onion, garlic and stock into a pan. Bring to the boil, cover and cook for 5 minutes, until the vegetables are tender. Remove the lid and boil until the stock has evaporated.

4 Rinse the aubergine and courgettes, drain and add to the pan, with the tomatoes and herbs. Cook for 10–12 minutes, until the aubergine and courgettes are tender, adding a little water if the mixture becomes too dry. Season to taste.

5 Meanwhile, bring a large pan of lightly salted water to the boil and cook the pasta until it is *al dente*. Drain thoroughly, return to the clean pan, and add the vegetable mixture and marinated beancurd, with any liquid left in the bowl. Toss lightly, then tip into a heated serving bowl and keep hot.

6 Spread out the remaining sesame seeds in a non-stick frying pan and quickly dry-fry them until golden. Sprinkle them over the pasta dish and serve.

Pasta with Roasted Pepper & Tomato Sauce

Add other vegetables, such as French beans, courgettes or even chick-peas, to make this delicious sauce even more substantial.

Serves 4

2 medium red peppers
2 medium yellow peppers
1 fresh red chilli, seeded
15ml/1 tbsp olive oil
1 medium onion, sliced
2 garlic cloves, crushed
400g/14oz can
　chopped tomatoes
10ml/2 tsp balsamic vinegar
450g/1lb/4 cups dried conchiglie
　or spirali
salt and freshly ground
　black pepper

1 Preheat the oven to 200°C/400°F/Gas 6. Spread out the peppers and chilli in a roasting tin, and roast for 30 minutes or until softened and beginning to char. Remove the tin from the oven and cover with several layers of kitchen paper.

2 Meanwhile, heat the oil in a non-stick pan. Add the onion and garlic, and cook over a low heat, stirring occasionally, for about 5 minutes, until soft and golden.

3 When the peppers and chilli are cool enough to handle, rub off the skins. Cut them in half, remove the seeds and chop the flesh roughly.

4 Stir the chopped peppers and chilli into the onion mixture, then add the tomatoes. Bring to the boil, lower the heat and simmer for 10–15 minutes until slightly thickened and reduced. Stir in the vinegar, and season to taste with salt and freshly ground black pepper.

5 Meanwhile, bring a large pan of lightly salted water to the boil and cook the pasta until *al dente*.

6 Drain the pasta well and add it to the sauce. Toss thoroughly to mix, then serve immediately in warmed bowls.

Tagliatelle with "Hit-the-pan" Salsa

It is possible to make a hot, filling meal within just 15 minutes with this quick-cook salsa sauce.

Serves 2

115g/4oz fresh tagliatelle
15ml/1 tbsp extra virgin olive oil
1 garlic clove, crushed
4 spring onions, sliced
1 green chilli, halved, seeded
　and sliced
3 tomatoes, chopped
juice of 1 orange
30ml/2 tbsp fresh
　parsley, chopped
salt and freshly ground
　black pepper
freshly grated strong hard
　cheese (optional)

1 Bring a large pan of lightly salted water to the boil and cook the pasta until it is *al dente*. Drain and place in a large bowl. Add about 5ml/1 tsp of the oil and toss to coat. Season well with salt and pepper.

2 Preheat a wok, swirl in the remaining oil and, when it is hot, stir-fry the garlic, onions and chilli for 1 minute. The pan should sizzle as they cook.

3 Add the tomatoes, orange juice and parsley. Season to taste with salt and pepper. Add the tagliatelle and toss over the heat until heated through. Divide among warmed individual plates and serve immediately with cheese, if using.

Cook's Tip
When squeezing citrus fruits, make sure that they are at room temperature, as they will then yield more juice than they would straight from the fridge.

Variation
You could use any pasta shape for this recipe. The sauce would be particularly good with large rigatoni or linguini and would also work well with filled fresh pasta, such as ravioli or tortellini.

Tagliatelle with Pea Sauce, Asparagus & Broad Beans

When you're tired of tomatoes, try this creamy pea sauce, which tastes great with a mixture of pasta and vegetables.

Serves 4

15ml/1 tbsp olive oil
1 garlic clove, crushed
6 spring onions, sliced
225g/8oz/2 cups frozen peas, thawed
350g/12oz fresh young asparagus, trimmed
30ml/2 tbsp chopped fresh sage, plus extra leaves to garnish
finely grated rind of 2 lemons
450ml/ ¾ pint/1 ¾ cups vegetable stock or water
225g/8oz/1 ½ cups frozen broad beans, thawed
450g/1lb fresh or dried tagliatelle
60ml/4 tbsp low-fat natural yogurt

1 Heat the oil in a pan. Add the garlic and spring onions, and cook over a low heat for 2–3 minutes, until softened.

2 Add the peas and one-third of the asparagus, together with the sage, lemon rind and stock or water. Bring to the boil, lower the heat and simmer for 10 minutes, until tender.

3 Transfer to a blender or food processor and process until smooth, then scrape the mixture into a pan. Pop the broad beans out of their skins and add them to the pan.

4 Cut the remaining asparagus into 5cm/2in lengths, trimming off any tough fibrous stems. Bring a large pan of lightly salted water to the boil, add the asparagus and cook for 2 minutes. Lift out with a slotted spoon and add to the pan of sauce. Reheat gently, stirring occasionally, while you cook the pasta.

5 Let the water return to the boil and add the tagliatelle. Cook until al dente.

6 Drain the pasta and return it to the clean pan. Add the yogurt and toss lightly. Divide among warmed plates and top with the sauce. Garnish with the extra sage leaves and serve.

Chinese Ribbons

This is a colourful Chinese-style dish, easily prepared using pasta instead of Chinese noodles.

Serves 4

1 medium carrot
2 small courgettes
175g/6oz runner or other green beans
175g/6oz baby corn cobs
450g/1lb dried ribbon pasta, such as tagliatelle
5ml/1 tsp sesame oil
15ml/1 tbsp corn oil
salt
1cm/½in piece of fresh root ginger, peeled and finely chopped
2 garlic cloves, finely chopped
90ml/6 tbsp yellow bean sauce
6 spring onions, sliced into 2.5cm/1in lengths
30ml/2 tbsp dry sherry
5ml/1 tsp sesame seeds

1 Slice the carrot and courgettes diagonally into chunks. Slice the beans diagonally. Cut the baby corn cobs diagonally in half.

2 Bring a large pan of lightly salted water to the boil and cook the pasta until it is al dente.

3 Drain the pasta well, return to the clean pan and add the sesame oil. Toss to coat.

4 Preheat a wok, then swirl in the corn oil. When it is hot, add the ginger and garlic, and stir-fry over a medium heat for 30 seconds, then add the carrots, beans, courgettes and corn cobs, and stir-fry for 3–4 minutes.

5 Stir in the yellow bean sauce. Stir-fry for 2 minutes, add the spring onions, sherry and pasta. Toss over the heat until piping hot. Divide among warmed bowls and serve immediately, sprinkled with sesame seeds.

Cook's Tip
Sesame oil has a strong nutty flavour and a distinctive aroma. It is generally used as a flavouring, rather than as a cooking oil.

Low-fat Tagliatelle with Mushrooms

Mushrooms cooked in stock, with wine and soy sauce have a superb flavour, and make a very good topping for fresh pasta. In addition, they contain no fat and no cholesterol at all.

Serves 4
1 small onion, finely chopped
2 garlic clove, crushed
150ml/ ¼ pint/ ⅔ cup
  vegetable stock
225g/8oz/3 cups mixed fresh
  mushrooms, quartered if large
60ml/4 tbsp white wine
10ml/2 tsp tomato purée
15ml/1 tbsp soy sauce
225g/8oz fresh sun-dried tomato
  and herb tagliatelle
5ml/1 tsp chopped fresh thyme
30ml/2 tbsp chopped
  fresh parsley
salt and freshly ground
  black pepper
shavings of strong hard cheese,
  to serve (optional)

1 Put the onion and garlic into a pan with the stock. Cover and cook over a medium heat for 10 minutes, or until tender.

2 Add the mushrooms, wine, tomato purée and soy sauce. Cover and cook for 5 minutes, then remove the lid from the pan and boil until the liquid has reduced by half.

3 Bring a large pan of lightly salted water to the boil and cook the pasta until it is *al dente*.

4 Meanwhile, stir the chopped fresh herbs into the mushroom mixture, and season with salt and pepper to taste.

5 Drain the pasta thoroughly, return it to the clean pan and add the mushroom mixture. Toss lightly and serve in warmed bowls, with the cheese, if you like.

Cook's Tip
Use cultivated or wild mushrooms, such as field, chestnut, oyster and chanterelle, or a mixture.

Tagliatelle with Spinach Gnocchi

Celebrate the sensible way with this sophisticated dish that looks and tastes indulgent but is relatively low in fat.

Serves 4–6
450g/1lb dried tagliatelle,
  preferably mixed colours
shavings of strong hard cheese,
  to garnish

For the spinach gnocchi
450g/1lb frozen chopped spinach
1 small onion, finely chopped
1 garlic clove, crushed
1.5ml/¼ tsp freshly
  grated nutmeg
400g/14oz/1¾ cups low-fat
  cottage cheese
115g/4oz/1 cup dried white
  breadcrumbs
flour, for dusting
75g/3oz/ ¾ cup semolina or
  plain flour
50g/2oz/ ⅔ cup freshly grated
  strong hard cheese
3 egg whites

For the tomato sauce
1 onion, finely chopped
1 celery stick, finely chopped
1 red pepper, seeded and diced
1 garlic clove, crushed
150ml/ ¼ pint/ ⅔ cup
  vegetable stock
400g/14oz can
  chopped tomatoes
15ml/1 tbsp tomato purée
10ml/2 tsp caster sugar
5ml/1 tsp dried oregano
salt and freshly ground
  black pepper

1 First, make the tomato sauce. Put the chopped onion, celery, pepper and garlic into a non-stick pan. Add the stock, bring to the boil and cook over a medium heat for 5 minutes, or until the vegetables are tender.

2 Stir in the tomatoes, tomato purée, sugar and oregano. Season to taste with salt and pepper, and bring to the boil. Lower the heat and simmer, stirring occasionally, for 30 minutes, until thickened.

3 Meanwhile, make the gnocchi. Put the frozen spinach, onion and garlic into a pan, cover and cook over a low heat until the spinach has thawed. Remove the lid and increase the heat to drive off any moisture. Season with salt, pepper and nutmeg to taste. Transfer the spinach mixture to a bowl and set aside to cool completely.

4 Add the cottage cheese, breadcumbs, semolina or flour, cheese and egg whites to the spinach mixture, and mix. Using two dessertspoons, shape the mixture into about 24 ovals and place them on a lightly floured tray. Place in the fridge for 30 minutes.

5 Bring a large shallow pan of lightly salted water to the boil, then lower the heat to a gentle simmer. Add the gnocchi in batches. As soon as they rise to the surface, after about 5 minutes, remove them with a slotted spoon and drain them thoroughly. Keep the cooked gnocchi hot.

6 Bring another large pan of salted water to the boil and cook the pasta until *al dente*. Drain thoroughly. Transfer to warmed serving plates, top with the spinach gnocchi and spoon over the tomato sauce. Scatter with shavings of strong hard cheese and serve at once.

Spinach & Hazelnut Lasagne

Lasagne is one of those dishes that almost everyone seems to like, and there will be plenty of takers for this low-fat vegetarian version.

Serves 4

900g/2lb fresh spinach leaves, stalks removed
300ml/ ½ pint/1¼ cups vegetable stock
1 medium onion, finely chopped
1 garlic clove, crushed

75g/3oz/ ¾ cup hazelnuts
30ml/2 tbsp chopped fresh basil
6 fresh lasagne sheets, precooked if necessary
400g/14oz can chopped tomatoes
200g/7oz/scant 1 cup low-fat fromage frais
salt and freshly ground black pepper
flaked hazelnuts and chopped fresh parsley, to garnish

1 Preheat the oven to 200°C/400°F/Gas 6. Wash the spinach and place it in a pan with just the water that clings to the leaves. Cover the pan and cook the spinach over a fairly high heat for 2 minutes, shaking the pan frequently, until it has wilted. Drain well.

2 Heat 30ml/2 tbsp of the stock in a large pan, add the chopped onion and garlic, and simmer until soft. Stir in the spinach, hazelnuts and basil.

3 In a large ovenproof dish, layer the spinach, lasagne sheets and tomatoes, seasoning each layer well. Pour over the remaining stock. Spread the fromage frais over the top.

4 Bake the lasagne for about 45 minutes, or until the topping is golden brown. Serve hot, sprinkled with lines of flaked hazelnuts and chopped parsley.

> **Cook's Tip**
> *The hazelnuts will taste even better if they are toasted. Spread them in a grill pan and grill them until golden. Tip them into a clean dish towel and rub off the skins.*

Aubergine & Mixed Vegetable Lasagne

Rather like a combination of lasagne and moussaka, this low-fat supper dish is quite filling, so it needs no accompaniment other than a small side salad.

Serves 6–8

1 large onion, finely chopped
2 garlic cloves, crushed
150ml/ ¼ pint/ ⅔ cup vegetable stock
1 small aubergine, cubed
225g/8oz/3 cups mushrooms, sliced
400g/14oz can chopped tomatoes
30ml/2 tbsp tomato purée
150ml/ ¼ pint/ ½ cup red wine

1.5ml/ ¼ tsp ground ginger
5ml/1 tsp mixed dried herbs
25g/1oz/2 tbsp low-fat spread
25g/1oz/ ¼ cup plain flour
300ml/ ½ pint/1¼ cups skimmed milk
a large pinch of freshly grated nutmeg
10–12 fresh lasagne sheets, precooked if necessary
200g/7oz/scant 1 cup low-fat cottage cheese
1 egg, beaten
25g/1oz/ ¼ cup grated reduced-fat Cheddar cheese
30ml/2 tbsp freshly grated strong hard cheese
salt and freshly ground black pepper

1 Put the onion and garlic into a heavy-based saucepan with the stock. Cover and cook over a medium heat for about 10 minutes, or until tender.

2 Add the aubergine cubes, sliced mushrooms, tomatoes, tomato purée, wine, ginger and herbs. Bring to the boil, cover and cook for 15–20 minutes. Remove the lid and cook over a high heat to evaporate the liquid by half. Season to taste with salt and pepper.

3 Put the low-fat spread, flour, skimmed milk and nutmeg into a pan. Whisk together over a medium heat until thickened and smooth. Season with salt and pepper to taste.

4 Preheat the oven to 200°C/400°F/Gas 6. Spoon about one-third of the vegetable mixture into the base of an ovenproof dish. Cover with a layer of lasagne and one-quarter of the sauce.

5 Make two more layers in the same way, then cover with the cottage cheese. Beat the egg into the remaining sauce and pour it over the top.

6 Sprinkle with the Cheddar and strong hard cheese, and bake for 25–30 minutes, or until the top is golden brown. Leave to stand for about 10 minutes before serving.

> **Variation**
> *Add some soaked porcini mushrooms to intensify the flavour, or cheat with a splash of good-quality mushroom ketchup.*

Pappardelle & Provençal Sauce

The flavours of the south of France are captured in this simple dish.

Serves 4

2 small red onions, peeled
150ml/ ¼ pint/ ⅔ cup
   vegetable stock
1–2 garlic cloves, crushed
60ml/4 tbsp red wine
2 courgettes, cut into fingers
1 yellow pepper, seeded
   and sliced
400g/14oz can
   chopped tomatoes
10ml/2 tsp chopped fresh thyme
5ml/1 tsp caster sugar
350g/12oz fresh pappardelle
salt and freshly ground
   black pepper
fresh thyme and 6 stoned black
   olives, roughly chopped,
   to garnish

1 Cut each onion into eight wedges, leaving the root end intact to hold them together during cooking. Put into a pan with the stock and garlic. Bring to the boil, lower the heat, cover and simmer for 5 minutes, until tender.

2 Add the red wine, courgettes, yellow pepper, tomatoes, chopped thyme and caster sugar, and season with salt and pepper to taste. Bring to the boil and cook over a low heat for 5–7 minutes, gently shaking the pan occasionally to coat all the vegetables with the sauce.

3 Meanwhile, bring a large pan of lightly salted water to the boil and cook the pasta until it is *al dente*.

4 Drain the pasta well, tip it into a warmed serving dish and top with the vegetable mixture. Garnish with the fresh thyme and chopped black olives, and serve immediately.

Cook's Tip
When making the sauce, do not overcook the vegetables, as the dish is much nicer if they have a slightly crunchy texture to contrast with the tender pasta.

Sweet & Sour Peppers with Farfalle

This Moroccan-inspired recipe has unusual ingredients, but the combination of flavours works very well.

Serves 4–6

1 red pepper
1 yellow pepper
1 orange pepper
1 garlic clove, crushed
30ml/2 tbsp drained
   bottled capers
30ml/2 tbsp raisins
5ml/1 tsp wholegrain mustard
grated rind and juice of 1 lime
5ml/1 tsp clear honey
30ml/2 tbsp chopped
   fresh coriander
225g/8oz/2 cups dried farfalle
salt and freshly ground
   black pepper
shavings of strong hard cheese,
   to serve (optional)

1 Cut the peppers into quarters, at the same time removing the stalks and seeds. Bring a large pan of water to the boil. Add the peppers and cook over a medium heat for 10–15 minutes, until tender.

2 Drain, rinse under cold water and drain again. Peel away the skin and cut the flesh lengthways into strips.

3 Put the garlic, capers, raisins, mustard, lime rind and juice, honey and coriander into a bowl and whisk together. Season with salt and pepper to taste.

4 Bring a large pan of lightly salted water to the boil and cook the pasta until it is *al dente*.

5 Drain the pasta thoroughly, return it to the clean pan and add the reserved peppers and dressing. Toss over a low heat for 1–2 minutes, then tip into warmed serving bowls. Serve with a few shavings of cheese, if using.

Spinach Ravioli Crescents

Impress your guests with these pretty pasta pasties filled with vegetables and cottage cheese.

Serves 4–6

1 bunch of spring onions, finely chopped
1 carrot, coarsely grated
2 garlic cloves, crushed
200g/7oz/scant 1 cup low-fat cottage cheese
15ml/1 tbsp chopped fresh dill, plus extra to garnish
25g/1oz/ ⅓ cup freshly grated strong hard cheese
6 halves sun-dried tomatoes, finely chopped
1 quantity of Basic Pasta Dough, flavoured with spinach
beaten egg white, for brushing
flour, for dusting
salt and freshly ground black pepper

1 Put the spring onions, carrot, garlic and cottage cheese into a bowl. Add the chopped dill and strong hard cheese, then stir in two-thirds of the chopped sun-dried tomatoes. Season to taste with salt and pepper, and set aside.

2 Roll the spinach pasta into thin sheets and cut it into 7.5cm/3in rounds with a fluted ravioli or pastry cutter.

3 Place a spoon of filling in the centre of each pasta round. Brush the edges with egg white, then fold each round in half to make crescents. Press the edges together to seal. Transfer to a floured dish towel to rest for 1 hour before cooking.

4 Bring a large pan of lightly salted water to the boil and cook the crescents in batches until they are just tender. Drain well.

5 Place the crescents on warmed serving plates and sprinkle over the remaining sun-dried tomatoes. Garnish with the extra chopped dill. Serve immediately.

Cook's Tip
Spinach-flavoured pasta not only looks pretty and complements the other ingredients, but it also seals better than plain pasta.

Vegetarian Cannelloni

Cannelloni is great for entertaining as it can be prepared in advance and popped into the oven when guests arrive.

Serves 4–6

1 onion, finely chopped
2 garlic cloves, crushed
2 carrots, coarsely grated
2 celery sticks, finely chopped
150ml/ ¼ pint/ ⅔ cup vegetable stock
115g/4oz/ ½ cup red lentils
400g/14oz can chopped tomatoes
30ml/2 tbsp tomato purée
2.5ml/½ tsp ground ginger
5ml/1 tsp chopped fresh thyme
5ml/1 tsp chopped fresh rosemary
40g/1½oz/3 tbsp low-fat spread
40g/1½oz/ ⅓ cup plain flour
600ml/1 pint/2½ cups skimmed milk
1 bay leaf
a large pinch of freshly grated nutmeg
16–18 cannelloni tubes
25g/1oz/ ¼ cup grated reduced-fat Cheddar cheese
25g/1oz/ ⅓ cup freshly grated strong hard cheese
25g/1oz/ ½ cup fresh white breadcrumbs
salt and freshly ground black pepper
flat leaf parsley, to garnish

1 Put the onion, garlic, carrots, celery and half the stock into a saucepan, cover and cook for 10 minutes, until tender. Add the lentils, tomatoes, tomato purée, ginger, thyme and rosemary. Stir in the remaining stock. Bring to the boil, lower the heat, cover and simmer for 20 minutes. Remove the lid and cook for about 10 minutes, until thick. Leave to cool.

2 Put the low-fat spread, flour, milk and bay leaf into a pan, and whisk over a medium heat until thick and smooth. Season with salt, pepper and nutmeg. Discard the bay leaf.

3 Preheat the oven to 180°C/350°F/Gas 4. Spoon the lentil filling into the cannelloni. Spoon half the white sauce into the base of an ovenproof dish. Arrange the cannelloni in a single layer on top and spoon over the remaining sauce to cover.

4 Mix the cheeses and breadcrumbs, then scatter over the cannelloni. Bake for 30–40 minutes. Garnish and serve.

Spaghetti with Mixed Bean Chilli

Chick-peas and three different types of bean make this a hearty dish, ideal for coming home to after a long walk on a winter's day.

Serves 6
1 onion, finely chopped
1–2 garlic cloves, crushed
1 large fresh green chilli, seeded and chopped
150ml/ ¼ pint/ ⅔ cup vegetable stock
400g/14oz can chopped tomatoes
30ml/2 tbsp tomato purée
120ml/4fl oz/ ½ cup red wine
5ml/1 tsp dried oregano
200g/7oz French beans, sliced
400g/14oz can red kidney beans, drained
400g/14oz can cannellini beans, drained
400g/14oz can chick-peas, drained
450g/1lb dried spaghetti
salt and freshly ground black pepper

1 Put the chopped onion, garlic and chilli into a non-stick pan and pour in the stock. Bring to the boil and cook over a medium heat for 10 minutes, until the onion is tender.

2 Stir in the tomatoes, tomato purée, wine and oregano, and season with salt and pepper to taste. Bring to the boil, lower the heat, cover and simmer the sauce for 20 minutes.

3 Cook the French beans in boiling, salted water for about 5–6 minutes, until tender. Drain thoroughly.

4 Add all the beans and the chick-peas to the sauce, and simmer for a further 10 minutes. Meanwhile, bring a large pan of lightly salted water to the boil and cook the spaghetti until *al dente*. Drain thoroughly. Transfer to a serving dish and top with the chilli. Serve immediately.

Cook's Tip
Use a packet of chilli seasoning mix instead of the fresh chilli, if you like. Simply stir it into the sauce with the tomatoes.

Stir-fried Noodles with Beansprouts

A classic Chinese noodle dish that makes a marvellous accompaniment.

Serves 4
175g/6oz dried egg noodles
15ml/1 tbsp vegetable oil
1 garlic clove, finely chopped
1 small onion, halved and sliced
225g/8oz/4 cups beansprouts
1 small red pepper, seeded and cut into strips
1 small green pepper, seeded and cut into strips
2.5ml/ ½ tsp salt
1.5ml/ ¼ tsp freshly ground white pepper
30ml/2 tbsp light soy sauce

1 Bring a pan of lightly salted water to the boil and cook the noodles until they are just tender, checking the packet for information on timing. Drain, rinse under cold water and drain well again.

2 Preheat a wok and swirl in the oil. When it is hot, add the garlic, stir briefly, then add the onion slices. Stir-fry for 1 minute over a medium heat, then add the beansprouts and peppers, and stir-fry for 2–3 minutes.

3 Stir in the drained noodles and toss over the heat, using two spatulas or wooden spoons, for 2–3 minutes or until the ingredients are well mixed and have heated through.

4 Add the salt, pepper and soy sauce, and stir thoroughly before serving the noodle mixture in warmed bowls.

Cook's Tip
White pepper comes from peppercorns that have ripened fully, unlike green or black peppercorns. The skin and outer flesh have been removed. White pepper is hot but not so aromatic as black pepper.

Five-spice Vegetable Noodles

Spicy, with delicious warmth from the chilli, ginger, cinnamon and other spices, this is exactly the right dish to serve for supper on a cold winter's evening.

Serves 2–3
225g/8oz dried egg noodles
2 carrots
1 celery stick
1 small fennel bulb
15ml/1 tbsp vegetable oil
2 courgettes, halved and sliced
1 fresh red chilli, seeded and chopped, plus sliced red chilli to garnish (optional)
2.5cm/1in piece of fresh root ginger, grated
1 garlic clove, crushed
7.5ml/1½ tsp Chinese five-spice powder
2.5ml/½ tsp ground cinnamon
4 spring onions, sliced
60ml/4 tbsp warm water

1 Bring a large pan of lightly salted water to the boil and cook the noodles briefly until they are just tender, checking the packet for information on timing. Drain, rinse under cold water and drain again.

2 Cut the carrots and celery stick into julienne. Cut the fennel bulb in half and cut out the hard core. Cut the flesh into slices, then into julienne.

3 Preheat a wok and swirl in the oil. When it is hot, add the carrots, celery, fennel, courgettes and chilli, and stir-fry over a medium heat for 7–8 minutes.

4 Add the ginger and garlic, and stir-fry for 2 minutes, then stir in the Chinese five-spice powder and cinnamon, and stir-fry for 1 minute more.

5 Add the spring onions and stir-fry for 1 minute. Moisten with the warm water and cook for 1 minute more.

6 Add the noodles, and toss and stir over the heat until well mixed and heated through. Divide the noodles among warmed individual bowls, garnish with sliced fresh red chilli, if liked, and serve immediately.

Beancurd Stir-fry with Egg Noodles

The sauce for this stir-fry is absolutely delicious, and the marinated beancurd adds both substance and an interesting contrast in texture.

Serves 4
225g/8oz firm smoked beancurd (tofu)
45ml/3 tbsp dark soy sauce
30ml/2 tbsp red vermouth
225g/8oz medium dried egg noodles
10ml/2 tsp clear honey
10ml/2 tsp cornflour
3 leeks, thinly sliced
2.5cm/1in piece of root ginger, finely grated
1–2 fresh red chillies, seeded and sliced into rings
1 small red pepper, seeded and thinly sliced
150ml/¼ pint/⅔ cup vegetable stock
salt and freshly ground black pepper

1 Cut the beancurd into 2cm/¾in cubes. Put it into a bowl with the soy sauce and vermouth. Toss well to coat, then set aside to marinate for 30 minutes.

2 Bring a large pan of lightly salted water to the boil and cook the noodles briefly until they are just tender. Drain, rinse under cold water and drain again.

3 Lift the beancurd from the marinade. Reserve the marinade and fry the beancurd quickly in a non-stick frying pan until lightly golden brown on all sides. Remove from the heat. Mix the honey and cornflour into the marinade and set it aside.

4 Put the leeks, ginger, chilli, pepper and stock into a large pan. Bring to the boil and cook over a high heat for 2–3 minutes, until the vegetables are crisp-tender.

5 Add the reserved marinade to the vegetable mixture and cook over a high heat, stirring constantly, until it thickens. Add the noodles and beancurd, and toss over the heat until both have heated through. Season to taste with salt and pepper.

6 Divide the stir-fry and noodles among warmed individual plates and serve immediately.

Noodles Primavera

As tasty as it is colourful, this is a substantial dish destined to become a favourite with all the family.

Serves 4
225g/8oz dried broad
   rice noodles
115g/4oz/scant 1 cup
   broccoli florets
1 carrot, thinly sliced lengthways
225g/8oz asparagus, trimmed
   and cut into 5cm/2in lengths
1 red or yellow pepper, seeded
   and cut into strips

50g/2oz baby corn cobs
50g/2oz/ ½ cup sugar snap peas,
   topped and tailed
30ml/2 tbsp vegetable oil
15ml/1 tbsp chopped fresh
   root ginger
2 garlic cloves, chopped
2 spring onions, finely chopped
450g/1lb tomatoes, chopped
1 bunch of rocket leaves
soy sauce, to taste
salt and freshly ground
   black pepper

1 Soak the noodles in hot water for about 30 minutes, until soft. Drain.

2 Bring a large pan of lightly salted water to the boil and blanch the broccoli florets for 1 minute. Lift out with a slotted spoon, refresh under cold water, drain and set aside.

3 Repeat this process in turn with the carrot, asparagus, red or yellow pepper, baby corn cobs and sugar snap peas, keeping all the vegetables separate.

4 Preheat a wok, add the oil and swirl it around. Add the ginger, garlic and spring onions, and stir-fry for 30 seconds over a medium heat. Then add the tomatoes and stir-fry for 2–3 minutes.

5 Add the noodles to the wok and toss over the heat for 3 minutes to heat through. Toss in the blanched vegetables and rocket leaves. Season with soy sauce, salt and pepper to taste, and cook, stirring and tossing all the time, until the vegetables are tender and the dish is piping hot. Transfer to a warmed serving bowl and serve immediately.

Oriental Vegetable Noodles

Fresh shiitake mushrooms and sesame oil are authentic oriental ingredients in this tasty stir-fry, but it is Italian balsamic vinegar that gives it the edge.

Serves 6
500g/1¼lb fine dried egg noodles
1 red onion

115g/4oz/1½ cups fresh
   shiitake mushrooms
15ml/1 tbsp vegetable oil
45ml/3 tbsp dark soy sauce
15ml/1 tbsp balsamic vinegar
10ml/2 tsp caster sugar
5ml/1 tsp salt
5ml/1 tsp sesame oil
celery leaves, to garnish

1 Bring a large saucepan of lightly salted water to the boil. Add the egg noodles and cook briefly until they are just tender. Drain thoroughly.

2 Thinly slice the red onion and the shiitake mushrooms. Preheat a wok, then add the vegetable oil and swirl it around. When the oil is hot, add the onion and mushrooms, and stir-fry for 2 minutes.

3 Add the noodles to the wok with the soy sauce, balsamic vinegar, sugar and salt. Toss them over the heat for 2–3 minutes, then add the sesame oil. Transfer to a warmed bowl and serve at once, garnished with the celery leaves.

> **Cook's Tip**
> Shiitake mushrooms have a unique flavour and texture. Originating in the East, they are now widely cultivated in Europe and the United States. The caps are velvety and tan in colour, sometimes with light veins or faint white spots. The stems are often quite tough and may need to be removed before cooking. Otherwise, simply wipe the mushrooms with kitchen paper. Do not wash them otherwise they will absorb more moisture. There is also no need to peel them. Shiitake mushrooms should be cooked gently and briefly, as prolonged cooking tends to make them tough and unpalatable.

Spicy Vegetable Chow Mein

Ten minutes is all the time it takes to make this simply delicious snack.

Serves 3
225g/8oz dried egg noodles
115g/4oz French beans
30ml/2 tbsp vegetable oil
2 garlic cloves, crushed
1 onion, chopped
1 small red pepper, seeded and chopped
1 small green pepper, seeded and chopped
1 celery stick, finely chopped
2.5ml/ ½ tsp Chinese five-spice powder
1 vegetable stock cube, crumbled
2.5ml/ ½ tsp freshly ground black pepper
15ml/1 tbsp soy sauce
salt

1 Bring a large pan of lightly salted water to the boil and cook the noodles briefly until they are just tender. Drain and spread out on a large plate to cool.

2 Blanch the French beans in lightly salted boiling water for 1 minute, then remove and drain.

3 Preheat a wok. Swirl in the oil and stir-fry the French beans, garlic, onion, peppers and celery, tossing them together to mix.

4 Stir in the five-spice powder and crumble in the stock cube. Stir in the black pepper and cook for 3 minutes.

5 Stir in the noodles and soy sauce. Toss the mixture over the heat for 2–3 minutes, until the noodles have heated through and are coated in the sauce. Transfer to a warmed serving bowl and serve at once.

> **Cook's Tip**
> Chinese five-spice powder is a mixture of star anise, pepper, fennel, cloves and cinnamon. It is available from supermarkets and Chinese food stores. When buying, make sure you have Chinese powder, as Indian five-spice powder is different.

Chow Mein with Cashew Nuts

It is the lemon sauce that makes this chow mein extra special.

Serves 4
225g/8oz dried egg noodles
15ml/1 tbsp vegetable oil
50g/2oz/ ½ cup cashew nuts
2 carrots, cut into matchsticks
3 celery sticks, cut into matchsticks
1 green pepper, seeded and cut into thin strips
225g/8oz/4 cups beansprouts
salt
30ml/2 tbsp toasted sesame seeds, to garnish

For the lemon sauce
30ml/2 tbsp light soy sauce
15ml/1 tbsp dry sherry
150ml/ ¼ pint/ ⅔ cup vegetable stock
grated rind and juice of 2 lemons
15ml/1 tbsp granulated sugar
10ml/2 tsp cornflour

1 Stir all the ingredients for the lemon sauce together in a jug. Bring a large pan of lightly salted water to the boil and cook the noodles until they are just tender. Drain and spread out on a plate to dry.

2 Preheat a wok and swirl in the oil. Add the cashew nuts, toss them quickly over a high heat until golden, then remove them with a slotted spoon and drain on kitchen paper.

3 Add the carrots and celery to the wok, and stir-fry over a medium heat for 4–5 minutes. Add the green pepper and beansprouts, and stir-fry for 2–3 minutes more.

4 Using a slotted spoon or spider, lift the vegetables out of the wok and set them aside on a plate. Pour the lemon sauce mixture into the wok and cook, stirring constantly, for about 2 minutes, until it is thick.

5 Return the vegetables to the pan, add the noodles and toss over the heat until heated through.

6 Finally, add the cashew nuts and toss them with the noodles and vegetables. Serve immediately on heated plates, with the toasted sesame seeds sprinkled on top.

Index